To Bill:-

Happy 75th = July 28, 1992

Love

Pauline —

Oh! To have wings,

to soar like the Eagle...

Avian Dreamers

by **Jerry Gildemeister**

with Photographic Illustration and Design by **Gildemeister**
and Oil Painting Illustrations by **Tim Larson**

A Bear Wallow Limited Edition Printing

Wagon train pioneers were still trekking westward
when man's dreams of flying finally became reality.

The Bear Wallow Publishing Company

It was on December 17, 1903 at Kitty Hawk, North Carolina when two bicycle-building brothers from Dayton, Ohio made the first powered flight in history. Wilbur and Orville Wright set the stage that day for exploring the new frontier, but as incredible as it seems, flight just didn't catch on in America. The nation was full of skeptics, and it was rare to find anyone ready to believe that man would ever fly. It took the inventiveness and determination of a few like the Wrights who saw the possibilities of space exploration in imagined terms and made their dreams come true.

Avian Dreamers *is our tribute to those men and women who pioneered the skies to begin our reach into the galaxies beyond.....*

Cathy Gildemeister
The Bear Wallow Publishing Company

Avian Dreamers

CONTENTS

* * *

Chapter

1

Flights of Fantasy

Down through history, winged objects have appeared in legends, fables, and religions throughout the world. The winged bulls of Assyria, flying chariots of the Far East, the winged god of Mercury, flying carpets of Arabia, witches on broomsticks, and angels in heaven are but a few examples that illustrate man's obsession with flight. But there can be little doubt that his desire for wings is largely due to his envy of birds, which were not only his chief source of inspiration to take to the air, but also a model on which to base his own efforts.

No one knows just when the mythical lure of the skies changed into reality. And it is little wonder that there were so many disasters. Until quite modern times, man had no conception of what made flight possible. It seemed that the early approach was to mimic the feathered creatures. Perhaps the most famous of these imitators was depicted by the legend of Icarus, whose father, Daedalus, made him a pair of wings to escape from the isle of Crete. Flying so high that the sun's heat melted the wax by which the wings were fastened, Icarus fell to his death in the sea far below.

Evidence shows that the earliest of civilizations were familiar with concepts of aeronautics through their use of arrows and boomerangs; and the Chinese were flying kites as early as 1,000 B.C., but the development of manned flight is often more fascinating than mythology.

Reliable records of man's attempts to fly come from medieval times when the so-called tower jumpers began to practice their rather grim flights of fancy and fantasy. Among the more noted was a twelfth century Saracen of Constantinople who donned a large cloak and lept from a tower, his only reward being a broken body and a premature death.

Leonard de Vinci, one of the world's great thinkers of the fifteenth century, was the first man to give the problem of human flight serious consideration. His insatiable appetite for knowledge led him to study the anatomy and structure of bird's wings and their movements in flapping flight. He recognized that gliding motion differed from flapping maneuvers, but most of his work concentrated on flapping-winged aircraft powered by human muscle, not realizing that sustained man-powered flight would probably never work to great satisfation. Though he demonstrated great imagination, and his sketch books were filled with drawings of ingenious, though quite impractical, ornithopters and helicopters, he spent no time in testing theories so he could learn from his mistakes. Nevertheless, he was far ahead of his time, and in spite of all his research and design, his work remained virtually unknown until the late 1800s.

For the next two centuries there were still many misguided souls who tried flying with some sort of winged implement, resulting only in more battered bodies through deathly crashes. Perhaps one of the most celebrated demonstrations was in Paris in 1742 when the Marquis de Bacqueville fastened wings to his arms and legs and lept from a rooftop in an attempt to fly across the river Seine. A large crowd gathered, only to see him flounder in the air, and fall into a washer woman's barge! He broke a leg and no doubt sorely fractured his pride, unable to understand the central truth of flight: man is not designed to fly like a bird. In marked contrast to feathered creatures, his heavy bone structure and weak chest muscles are well designed for movement on earth and in the water, but quite ill-suited to skyward venturing.

The histories of seventeenth and eighteenth century flight disclose more dreamers working on a variety of outlandish schemes, from aerial boats with copper spheres and sails to bird-powered contraptions. But, on November 21, 1783 there was a turning point, a major contribution to the future of flight when Pilatre de Rozier and a French major made the first free flight over Paris in a hot air balloon developed by Joseph and Etienne Mongolfier. This sensational event prompted a wave of balloon mania that eventually had a profound affect on fixed-winged navigation. Not only were these new balloons alternative means of aerial transportation, they were used as testing rigs for parachutes, propellers, and aero-engines.

The development of the Montgolfier balloon fired the imagination of Sir George Cayley, who was only ten years old at the time. Until his death in 1857 he devoted all his energies to the theory and practice of flight, predicting that, "Aerial navigation will form the most prominent feature in the progress of civilization." He constructed a five-foot-long model glider in 1804, and five years later launched a full-sized model which flew a short distance, carrying a spunky boy. After working on a variety of inventive flying machines, he returned to working on gliders, and in 1853 he constructed a full-sized triplane with built-in longitudinal and lateral stability, plus pilot-operated elevator and rudder control. His reluctant coachman was persuaded to fly across the valley at Brompton, England to make the first gliding flight in history. Cayley anticipated in almost every way the aeroplane of the twentieth century and expressed his firm conviction that "this noble art will soon be brought home to man's convenience, and that we will be able to transport ourselves and families and their goods and chattels more securely by air than by water and with a velocity of from 20 to 100 miles per hour." Sadly, in spite of his accurate predictions and brilliant research, Cayley's work was all but ignored for decades, but in more recent times historians have considered him the true inventor of the aeroplane.

In the mid-1800s balloons were still in vogue, but the subject of winged flight was regarded with skepticism and ridicule by the general public. This was hardly surprising since the flappers still seemed bent on mastering the skies, and the industry seemed to be dominated by eccentrics, charlatans, and a variety of other questionable showmen.

One of the more bizarre developments of the era was a steam flapper designed around 1830 by Englishman F.D. Artingstall. Encouraged by the progress of railway steam engines, he built a full-sized steam-powered ornithopter with four wings flapping alternately like a giant dragonfly. Experiencing the same fate as a previous model, this one flapped itself to pieces and exploded, thus putting an end to Artingstall's dream. Predictably, though, others caught his dream and sustained it to another interesting chapter in the history of aerial transportation.

There is no question that the experimentation of Otto and Gustave Lilienthal had profound effects on the future of aeronautics. As boys, the two brothers marveled at the ability of the birds which flew over their home on the edge of the Baltic Sea.

They grew up to pursue differing careers, but neither quit thinking of the possibility of manned flight. Otto trained as an engineer and designed mining equipment, while Gustave worked as an architect and builder. Shortly after Gustave's return from work in Australia, they began experimenting in earnest, building gliders and taking short hops from their man-made hill. Otto did most of the flying, as he was the most muscular of the two and could better control the direction of his descent by bending and manipulating the glider's wings. He was meticulous in his record-keeping, faithfully recording the results of his performance after each of more than two thousand glides.

On Sunday, August 9, 1896, Otto went to the proving ground with an assistant, forgetting a shock absorber which had saved his life on several occasions. He took off into the wind, and was gliding at quite a height when he seemed to stop dead in mid-air. He had experienced this situation several times before, but by shifting his weight, had been able to continue in flight. This time the glider slowly nosed down, then suddenly plunged to earth, throwing Otto clear. He was unconcious when his assistant picked him up and carried him to a local inn where he regained conciousness, but never made it through the night. Though he met an untimely death, Otto Lilienthal made his mark on aviation by becoming the father of modern-day hang-gliding.

An outstanding aeronautical figure in America during the late 1800s was the French-born civil engineer, Octave Chanute, whose interest in aviation began well before Lilienthal's gliding experiments in Germany. In his home town of Chicago, he carried out exhaustive investigation into heavier-than-air flight, collecting every available bit of information he could find. In 1894 he published a series of articles that were eventually reprinted in a book called ***Progress in Flying Machines***, which was to provide others with a wealth of documentation for their experimentation.

During this same period Professor Samuel P. Langley, an American scientist, engineer, astronomer, and director of the Smithsonian Institution in Washington, D.C., had already successfully flown scale models of steam and petrol-driven aircraft for up to three-quarters of a mile. In 1898 the United States government had granted him $50,000 to develop a full-sized machine based on the design of his successful models. After four years of development, and one failed test in the fall of 1903, he was ready to launch his flying boat, the *Aerodrome*.

By late afternoon on December 8, 1903, the hydroplane was in position on a catapult launch mounted on the top of Langley's houseboat which was moored on the edge of the Potomac River. The wind was gusting up to 20 miles per hour and winter darkness was not far away as Charles Manly, in his long underwear and cork-lined canvas jacket, climbed into the pilot's position and revved up the engine for a preflight check.

Observers from the War Department, reporters, a doctor, and assorted other onlookers hovered nearby. For Professor Langley, it was an almost unbearably suspenseful moment. He had devoted the last 17 years of his life to the development of a power-driven airplane, and the stakes were enormous: the *Aerodrome* just *had* to fly!

At 4:45 P.M. the catapult hurled the craft toward the darkening sky. The machine shot upward before it reached the end of the track, then it performed a half loop. Its tail twisted and crumpled, the *Aerodrome* dropped bottomside-up into the river within a few yards of the houseboat. Manly went down feet first, clinging to the sides of the cockpit as the machine pressed him underwater. His lifejacket snagged on a metal fitting, and it took all his strength to rip the garment and free himself before his lungs filled with the frigid river water. Then he dived, swam clear of the wreckage, and surfaced, only to strike his head on a chunk of floating ice. Shortly afterward he was hauled aboard the houseboat where he sputtered curses of disappointment while the doctor applied blankets and dosed him with whiskey. Once more the *Aerodrome* had been a dismal failure. The War Department quickly lost all interest in Langley and his dream, and withdrew all support, leaving him totally heartbroken.

Although Langley made little impression on the science of aviation, his enthusiasm and confidence in the future of powered flight led others to pursue their dreams of severing earth-bound bonds and taking wing to literally soar like an eagle.

Chapter

2

On Powered Wing

1902 Glider at Kitty Hawk

It is hard to believe that the interest still centered on balloons and airships when there was so much experimenting going on with heavier-than-air flying machines in the late 1800s. The general public and the so-called experts still considered the fixed-wing aeroplane a freak of man's indomitable imagination; there were two brothers who believed otherwise. Since their early childhood in Dayton, Ohio, Wilbur and Orville Wright were intrigued with flight and began constructing models before progressing to more serious study of aeronautics after the death of their hero, glider pioneer Otto Lilienthal who was killed while flying in 1896. Neither brother was educated beyond high school, but they both had inquiring minds and an active interest in mechanical flight, so it was natural that they sought out the writings of such authorities as Lilienthal, Cayley, Langley, and Chanute. Before long they arrived at some important new conclusions, and they were determined to find more efficient ways of maintaining control in the air while avoiding the dangers. They were going to gain flying experience without loss of life.

Like many of their predecessors, the Wrights watched birds to see how they managed the fluctuations of air currents. Their observations of the turkey vulture's soaring flight provided them with a clue. They noted that when the bird was laterally displaced by a gust of wind, it righted itself by torsion, or helical twistings of its wing-tips—if the leading edge of one tip was twisted downward, then the opposite wing had an upward turn. It made them wonder: if wings of an aircraft could be made to twist in a similar manner, the pilot could control and stabilize the aircraft in that same way, rather than by shifting his own body. To achieve this, the wings would have to be light enough to be warped, as they described it, and yet strong enough to lift the aircraft in the normal way.

After first trying out their wing-warping theory on a kite, Wilbur and Orville set about making their first glider in 1900—a biplane with a seventeen-foot wingspan and controllable elevator. The pilot was to lie prone to reduce air resistance and to minimize the chance of injury while landing. For added safety they decided to tether the aircraft during early trials to gain experience from prolonged flying time.

All that was lacking in this grand scheme was a location. After much study of wind and weather conditions, the brothers decided to conduct their tests near the small fishing village of Kitty Hawk, North Carolina which was noted for its strong and constant winds.

Their first trials were a success. Not only did the wing-warping device and elevator respond well, but the glider confirmed their belief in inherent instability. The Wrights returned home elated, more determined than ever to make a powered flight.

Through the winter they constructed a larger glider with a number of modifications, and the next summer they completed glides up to 389 feet, but found there were numerous problems. They now began to doubt Lilienthal's findings and other scientific data. After two years of experimentation they decided to rely entirely on their own investigations. Returning to their drawing boards, they started extensive research, including testing of wings in a wind tunnel. With renewed confidence, they developed their Number 3 Glider.

Their greatest improvement was the addition of a double fixed fin at the rear of the craft. Its purpose was to counteract the previous glider's alarming habit of slipping when warp was applied. Problems with the fixed fin were then solved by replacing it with a single movable rudder, with its control cables coupled to the warping mechanism. This combination of automatic control meant that the rudder would always move in the direction of the bank, thus counteracting warp-drag. This new machine made perfectly controlled glides in winds up to 35 mph and was at last able to perform smooth-banked turns, remaining sensitive and responsive to the lightest touch of the controls.

During the fall of 1902 the two brothers made nearly a thousand glides at Kitty Hawk, becoming experienced and skilled pilots in a comparatively short time. At the end of October they returned to Dayton, once again in high spirits. They wasted no time in getting back to designing a larger machine, operated this time by mechanical power. The only problem was that no power unit to meet their needs existed. Looking for a light, efficient engine or someone who would design them one, they wrote manufacturing companies but received no satisfactory answers, so they set about designing an engine and propellers with their own imaginative resources.

During the summer of 1903 the Wrights worked on their new model and then packed it off to Kitty Hawk. After arrival, weeks were spent on meticulous preparation and gliding practice with the old Number 3 Glider. Finally, on December 14th, after many mechanical breakdowns and exasperating setbacks, their *Flyer* was ready for its maiden flight. Early in the afternoon they tacked a signal flag to the hangar—a prearranged signal to the crew of the nearby Kill Devil lifesaving station that the aircraft was ready to fly. Five men arrived in time to help the brothers lay a track 150 feet up the sandy hillside and settle the machine up on it. The men from the station stood by as the brothers flipped a coin to see who would be first to fly. Wilbur won and climbed into position on the wing. With his brother holding the right wing-tip to steady the machine, Wilbur released the restraining wire. The *Flyer* raced down the track and shot 15 feet into the air by the time it was 100 feet from the end of the track. In his excitement he put on too much elevator, causing the plane to stall and then plough into the sand. Luckily the damage was light and the craft was repaired within a couple of days.

On the morning of the 17th, Orville slipped into the pilot's position to attempt their next launch. It was just nine days after Langley's second failure at powered flight, so anticipation was running high.

With no one from the press on hand, and only five witnesses, Wilbur steadied the wing of the *Flyer* as it sped down the track and took off into a 21-mph wind. Orville raised the elevator and the machine rose to about 10 feet, dipped, climbed again, then darted for the ground about 120 feet beyond the end of the track. Followed by the little band of spectators, Wilbur dashed across the windswept sand to the spot where the machine had skidded to a halt. He was the first to congratulate his brother on this momentous occasion. For twelve short seconds a machine carrying a man had risen into the air on its own, achieving full flight and landing safely.

The first to announce the news to the outside world was 18-year-old Johnny Moore who reached the Kitty Hawk Post Office and exclaimed, "They have done it! Damned if they ain't flew!" Very little appeared in print except for a few buried lines simply stating the Wright's declaration. The press had been burned too often with outlandish claims and did not bother to investigate, thus missing one of the greatest exclusives in history.

The brothers made three more flights that day. On the 4th flight Wilbur covered 852 feet and stayed aloft for 59 seconds before coming hard to the ground, damaging the elevator. Aided by the crew from the lifesaving station, the brothers tried to move the craft back to the shed for repair, but suddenly, without warning, a gust of wind flipped the craft over and tore it away from the handlers. Rolling over and over, the ship finally came to rest, smashed beyond immediate repair, ending that season of experimentation.

Later in the afternoon they sent a telegram to their father, informing him of their success. Then they prepared to pack up and return to Dayton, knowing that the age of the flying machine had come at last. Eventually the news made its way into the headlines, but the brothers did not elaborate or release any photographs, for they were worried about protecting a remarkable invention which they spent so long in developing, and entirely at their own expense.

By mid-1904 the *Flyer* was history. It was packed in crates and stored in a shed behind the Dayton workshop, and the *Flyer II* was often seen sailing serenely over Huffman Prairie, a cow pasture located about eight miles east of town. Now that the inventors had a successful, powered machine and degree of skill to handle it, they no longer needed the high winds and unlimited space of the Kitty Hawk site.

The brothers built a wooden hangar at the end of the Huffman pasture to house the new machine. They commuted daily from home to work with the *Flyer II* which was heavier, structurally stronger, and better powered than its predecessor; also, the wing camber was shallower and the elevator control relocated for easier handling.

Working now under the eyes of only an occasional friend or relative, the Wrights proceeded to test and refine their machine. Through the summer they made a number of trial flights over 1,300 feet, gaining valuable practice in handling a mechanized craft, and making improvements in the machine itself. With the help of a newly-developed launching device, they made 105 flights in 1904—their longest being five minutes and eight seconds, over a three mile distance, while flying in circles around the pasture.

Experiments and improvements continued through 1905. Finally, the brothers were satisfied that they had passed from mere scientific experimentation to the realm of useful application. On the forty-sixth flight of the season, Wilbur stayed aloft for thirty-eight minutes and three seconds, making thirty rounds of the field—over twenty-four miles! By then the 1905 *Flyer* was the world's first practical airplane. Not only could it stay in the air for more than a few minutes, but it could also bank, turn, and perform a figure eight.

By now Wilbur and Orville were confident enough to offer their invention to the nation. Continual experimentation was costly and the brothers hoped to be reimbursed for their painstaking work. They had not expected to profit financially in the early years of experiments; the distinction of being the first men to fly seemed reward enough. Now,

Flyer II at Huffman Prairie

however, they had begun to realize the practical application of their invention, and approached further development of the machine with an eye toward recouping something for their investment.

Wilbur wrote the U.S. Army three times in 1905, seeking support, but to no avail. He also wrote to his Congressman, offering to develop a practical *Flyer* for the United States government. The bureaucracy was slow to pick up on the idea, however, and by the end of the year the brothers decided to look elsewhere for a buyer, so Wilbur contacted the Ambassador of France.

Just as it seemed that their negotiations were in vain, their luck changed. In February of 1908 they were awarded a contract by the U.S. Signal Corps requiring a machine "capable of carrying two men and sufficient fuel supplies for a flight of 125 miles, with a speed of at least 40 miles an hour." Both the pilot and passenger were to be in a sitting position, so they would have to change their controls, but this would pose little problem and they promised delivery in two hundred days for $25,000. Six weeks later they also had a contract with a wealthy Frenchman who intended to form a syndicate to buy the rights to manufacture, sell, or license the use of the Wright machine in France. The pressure was on: they had two contracts to satisfy.

The brothers lost no time in getting to work, as both contracts had to be fullfilled simultaneously. By May of 1908 they were ready to test their redesigned machine, and on the 14th they made another historic breakthrough by taking a passenger on board.

That summer Wilbur sailed for France to demonstrate their *Flyer A*. On August 8th, in the cool, windless, near-twilight of a summer evening, he prepared to take off before a highly critical audience of Europeans—mostly French pilots who collectively considered themselves the leaders in aviation development and achievement.

But after Wilbur put the *Flyer A* through a series of climbs and banks with unbelievable perfection and grace, the crowd went wild with amazement. Instantly, Wilbur Wright was a hero—all of Europe was captivated by the quiet and unassuming Yankee aviator who had demonstrated the enormous technical lead he and his brother had over anyone else in the world.

By 1909 the lonely and secretive years were behind them. Now fame, honors, and material rewards were forthcoming and the Wright brothers were finally recognized as the true pioneers of modern flight.

Orville and Wilbur

Chapter

3

The Exhibition Years

Curtiss Pusher at Atlantic City

Since the Wright brothers had worked in relative obscurity and were obsessed with keeping the details of their invention secret, few people had heard of their achievement and fewer yet understood or believed what a remarkable feat had been accomplished. The other believers in flight, however, slowly and painfully reinvented the aeroplane, and one by one, followed the Wrights into the sky.

Close on their heels was Glenn Curtiss, the next American to build and fly an aeroplane. He started by building engines for bicycles, setting several speed records while racing motorcycles of his own design and manufacture, and, in 1904, contracting to build a powerplant for the U.S. Army's first dirigible. This led to an interest in aircraft and a long aeronautical career. In 1907 he joined Alexander Graham Bell and others to form the Aerial Experiment Association. On June 20, 1908, their *June Bug* biplane, with Curtiss at the controls, made a distance flight of 1,266 feet. Two weeks later Curtiss won the *Scientific American* trophy and generated news headlines by making the first official public flight of more than one mile, though this was not much of a contest as the Wrights chose not to compete. But the *June Bug's* success did have an impact on the aviation world— the Wrights, worried about protecting their invention, warned Curtiss about patent infringement, stating, "...if it is your desire to enter the exhibition business, we would be glad to take up the matter of license to operate under our patents for that purpose."

Curtiss brushed off the Wrights' letter with a qualified assurance that he was not intending to go into exhibition, then ignored the conflict by going on to merge his motorcycle and engine plant into the Herring-Curtiss Company, improving his pusher aircraft and developing the first seaplane which he flew off the water on January 26, 1911.

Glenn Curtiss piloting the June Bug

In spite of the marvelous achievements by the Wrights and Curtiss, flying just didn't catch on in America. The nation was full of skeptics, and the few people who did believe man could fly considered it only a novelty or a gadget for the rich, since a flying machine cost more than $5,000 to own.

In order to drum up interest in aviation, an enthusiastic Aeronautic Society of New York staged the world's first public exhibition of flying machines in November of 1908. The show was marginally successful. It succeeded in drawing 20,000 paying spectators, but as to advancing flight in the nation, it was a dismal flop. None of the machines were able to fly: there was a helicopter with twenty electric-fan blades, another flimsy machine with four sets of wings in tandem, and finally an immense biplane over ten feet tall with no sign of adequate power. All three machines were excused from flying on the grounds that they were still under construction! That left a special collection of kites the Society had assembled for the exhibition, but there wasn't enough wind to get any of them airborne. The planned balloon launch failed when the hydrogen-producing apparatus broke down, and the finale was a teenage boy riding a kite pulled by an automobile which crashed, breaking his ankle, sending him to the local hospital. Quite a show!

The costs of experimenting were becoming prohibitive so the inventors sought alternate sources of revenue to keep afloat. This brought the formation of exhibition companies and flying schools. The Wrights led the way in 1910 with flight schools in Montgomery, Alabama and at Huffman Prairie near their home town of Dayton. It wasn't long before Glenn Curtiss followed suit with schools at Hammondsport, New York and San Diego, California. Soon there was competition from others like John Moisant, Thomas Baldwin, Glenn Martin, and the Stinson family.

In order to get the jump on their competitors the Wrights hired Roy Knabenshue as their air show manager, and then hit the road with a crew of daredevil pilots, including:

Walter Brookins, Charlie Hamilton, Beckwith Havens, Charles Willard, Eugene Ely, and Lincoln Beachey.

The crowds who came to watch thought the pilots were a bunch of fakes; few were ready to believe that an aeroplane could actually fly. In fact, they were giving odds against it. But once they saw those marvelous machines buzzing overhead, they were crazed with excitement and even the worst skeptics suddenly became true believers.

The Wrights, Curtiss, Moisant, and a host of lesser American entrepreneurs hastened to capitalize on the popular new phenomenon. They scoured the countryside for brash young daredevils to tour the nation and to bring the first glimpse of an aeroplane to the masses. During the first exhibition year of 1910, the Wrights were charging $5,000 for each plane used, and the pilots received a base pay of $20 per week plus $50 per day when they flew. At those rates some pilots earned over $6,000 that season. The following year was the golden summer of exhibition flying, and the Curtiss Exhibition Company, starring a troupe of thirteen daredevil aviators, grossed nearly $1,000,000. There was no longer a question about the profitability of flying.

But the novelty of just seeing a flying machine sail around in the sky and perform a few maneuvers didn't last long. Crowds began demanding stunts of escalated recklessness for their money; pilots brave enough or crazy enough to push their machines to the limits to give the crowds what they wanted found their pay escalated accordingly. It wasn't long before some exhibition pilots were earning $1,000 for a day's work—provided, of course, that their planes held together under the strain and provided they survived to collect their earnings. Primitive flying fields were hazard enough, but high winds and more demanding crowds often proved to be a lethal combination. Exhibition flying became a profession that offered young daredevils adulation, excitement, and great riches, but an appallingly brief life expectancy. In 1910 more than thirty pilots tragically lost their lives.

But in spite of the carnage, flying rapidly became the craze of the nation, and increasing numbers of passengers and pilots took to the air. What had been solely a man's sport was now being discovered by women as a means of escaping into an exciting lifestyle. But few Americans were sympathetic to the idea of teaching women to fly, for the general concensus was that a woman's place was in the home raising a family, not roaming the carefree skies. One of the few who was sympathetic to their cause was Alfred Moisant who had no qualms about teaching "the weaker sex" to fly, and enrolled several into his school on Long Island.

Blanche Scott was the first woman to lead the way. She started out as an automobile driver, and made a daring cross-country trip in 1910—traveling in an Overland car from New York City to San Francisco. Then she got an introduction to flying from Glenn Curtiss before seeking further instruction from the Moisant School. By the summer of 1911 she was sharing the wind with the likes of Harriet Quimby and Matilde Moisant.

Oddly, one of the greatest problems facing women flyers was simply what to wear. For centuries, women's fashions seemingly had been styled to prevent them from stepping out of their limited roles and into more active competition with men. In the early 1900s, skirts dragged the ground, and corsets contorted the figure into exaggerated hourglass shapes. Even the slight raising of hemlines, which some thought scandalous, was far from the ideal outfit for making a flight in an open biplane. Harriet Quimby, known as the *Dresden China Aviatrice*, set the fashion world afire with her hightop leather boots and plum-colored satin costume consisting of buttoned knickerbockers and a blouse with a monkhood attached. She dazzled crowds with her exhibition flights around New York City, then she and Matilde Moisant made headlines in December of 1911 when they flew at the inauguration of the newly elected Mexican President Maderos.

The following year Harriet gained world-wide fame by being the first woman to fly the English Channel then, less than three months after after her triumph, she was dead, the victim of a bizarre accident.

While flying over Dorchester Bay, near Boston, her plane dropped suddenly, throwing her passenger from his seat. Without his weight the Bleriot flipped over, tossing Harriet out also. The two landed in about five feet of water, and both were instantly killed from the long plunge.

Soon other women were to share the headlines with their male counterparts—women like Katherine Stinson, who took to the airshow circuit in 1913, to captivate crowds with loops, inverted flying, and other dazzling aerial antics; and Ruth Law, a contemporary who performed as an exhibition flyer, and went on to set a long-distance solo flight record of 512 miles. The success of these and other pilots brought widespread attention to flying.

By 1914, the roster of aviators had grown from the two Wright brothers to more than 2,000 men and women who had taken to the air. With the lure of flight so irresistible, it was only natural that exhibition flying became commonplace at fairs and circuses around the nation. Organized flying meets became major spectator events attracting thousands of people in a single day. Many prominent figures became associated with these events, which did much to increase the prestige and acceptance of aviation in America.

As romantic as the flying machines might have seemed, they were still tricky to fly. Even with all of the improvements over the years, little yet was known about the real mysteries of flight. Most pilots learned early on that it was best to fly in the morning or late afternoon when the air was at its calmest. However, highfaluting promotion men, oblivious to the hazards of hot air, excessive winds, and severe turbulence, usually scheduled performances right after mid-day. Crowds insisted that the show start on time, regardless of weather conditions, and any pilot delay could easily incite a riot, as they would assume the whole deal was a fraud.

The glory of the era dimmed with the outbreak of fighting in Europe. It seemed that overnight all attention was shifted to the war effort, and the exhibition years of thrills and excitement were over, but there remained stories to tell and experiences to recall for the generations to come.....

Anything but Ordinary

Without question, probably the most foolhardy of all the exhibition flyers was Charlie Hamilton, a daredevil member of the Curtiss team.

At 110 pounds, with red hair, extruding ears, and dangling cigarette, he may never have fit the mold of the dashing young pilots, but he surely was one of the nerviest who ever plied the skies.

Charlie started his flying career early in life. Armed only with an umbrella, he jumped out the schoolhouse window in his hometown of New Britain, Connecticut. As he grew older he got a little wiser and started using a parachute, entertaining at fairs and circuses around the country, becoming one of the most daring chutists of all time. His most outstanding stunt was leaping from a balloon with a parachute and cutting loose from it, then opening and discarding a second one, then another, and another, and another, until he landed safely with his fifth and final chute.

In 1906 he switched to flying dirigibles, and then became interested in airplanes after Louis Bleriot's English Channel crossing and France's air meet at Rheims in 1909. In the fall of that year he went to Hammondsport, New York to see if Glenn Curtiss would teach him to fly, but Curtiss had not yet set up a flying school and told Hamilton he couldn't take him on as a student. Charlie hung around anyway, and when Curtiss left town on business, he climbed aboard a new plane while no one was looking and made several short flights without one bit of instruction! The next day he tried flying again and was caught by Curtiss who was furious that someone would risk a brand-new $5,000 aeroplane. But he was also impressed at Hamilton's demonstration of natural ability, and agreed to give him some private lessons.

Within a month Hamilton was good enough to join the Curtiss Exhibition flyers, and it wasn't long before he emerged as one of the most daring airmen in the nation. Once, for $10,000, he agreed to fly his plane up the narrow corridor of Broadway in New York City. The authorities stopped him, but more often than not he flew as he pleased—anywhere, anytime for money or just the sheer enjoyment of it.

One of Hamilton's most memorable flights was from New York City to Philadelphia. The ***New York Times*** and the ***Philadelphia Ledger*** offered a combined purse for a round trip flight between the two cities. Charlie couldn't resist the challenge and on the morning of June 13, 1910, he warmed up his Curtiss pusher for the cross-state journey. With him was the nation's first aerial mail—letters sent from New York's Governor Hughes and Mayor Gaynor to Pennsylvania's Governor Stuart and Philadelphia's Mayor Reyburn, plus a special message from the ***New York Times*** to the ***Philadelphia Ledger***. Around 7:00 A.M. he tried to lift off from Governor's Island, but the ground conditions were soft and the narrow tires of the biplane sank into the sand. One wheel came in contact with a long stick which flipped up to contact the whirring propeller. A giant splinter broke off of the wooden prop, causing a shut-down and flight delay until a replacement could be transferred from another plane. At 7:35 A.M. Hamilton was off again, this time without mishap. He headed over the harbor to meet up with his escort train. About nineteen miles out he was spotted by the engineer who notified Charlie's wife and mother who were aboard the train. It was a wonderous sight to everyone: Charlie and his biplane skimming directly above the tracks and straight ahead of the rushing locomotive, tilting gently, first to one side then the other, then rising and falling, riding on the crest of the wind.

At fifty miles an hour the two machines kept pace across the countryside, and then Hamilton and his plane gained a bit as the train passed over the Raritan River and through downtown New Brunswick. From then on Charlie kept the lead the rest of the way to Philadelphia, covering the eighty-five mile distance in an hour and fifty minutes—landing amidst the cheers of some 30,000 spectators gathered for the occasion.

After delivering the letters, accepting congratulations, and getting a bite to eat, he jumped in his machine and after a short run of around 100 feet, rose gracefully into the air, made a broad turn and headed straight for New York.

He was nearly seventy miles out when a cracked sparkplug caused one of the cylinders to skip, so reducing the engine power that a forced landing was imminent. The only spot available was a swampy opening which mired the machine. After fixing the broken plug, Hamilton struggled to get his plane to a bit of hard ground. Then, revving the motor and starting a takeoff, the rear wheels struck a mudhole, and as the machine sank, the propeller struck the ground and shattered. A passing motorist picked Charlie up and rushed him to a telephone so he could order a new propeller. A quick automobile trip from New York City brought him the new prop for a quick exchange, and at 6:10 P.M. he resumed his flight under the most trying of circumstances. Rising from a narrow road flanked by trees and telegraph poles, with not over six inches of clearance on either side, he lifted off for Governor's Island where he landed safely at 6:39 P.M. to claim the $10,000 prize money. He also set a new distance record—beating the record set by Glenn Curtiss just a month earlier.

Hamilton went on to set more records with his bravado, being the first to perform night flights and to popularize stunt flying. His favorite antic was the *Hamilton Glide* in which he would climb to an altitude of several hundred feet, cut his engine and propel the machine only with the force of gravity. In order to maintain flying speed, he descended at a fearful angle, continuing his dive nearly into the ground before leveling off to skim the surface with his wheels only a couple of feet from the earth before alighting.

Hamilton always flew with a daring sort of fatalism that awed his fellow pilots and led to more than the usual number of crashes. Many wondered how he managed to survive so long. He had broken both legs, smashed his collarbone twice, fractured two ribs, dislocated an arm, broken an ankle, and was badly scalded by hot water from his engine's radiator. He reportedly had two replacement ribs of silver, a metal plate in his shinbone, and another in his skull. All of this caused his fellow pilot Lincoln Beachey to remark, "There is little left of the original Hamilton."

Amazingly, Charlie Hamilton outlasted many of his contemporaries, and it was not an airplane that did him in; he suffered from tuberculosis, and died from a lung hemorrage on January 22, 1914.

A Year of Controversy and Tragedy

The success of the 1909 Rheims Air Show in France set off an aerial gold rush on both sides of the Atlantic. The lure of flight, quick fame, and great fortune triggered immense interest in aviation, and promoters wasted no time in jumping on the bandwagon when they could see there was big money to be made. Air tourneys were organized with purses of thousands of dollars, promising to attract aviators who had great box office appeal. The year of 1910 was destined to be a memorable one in the annals of American aviation.

The largest meet of the year was to be held in the fall of the year at Belmont Park on Long Island, but from the start it was marked by controversy. The Wright brothers had patent-infringement suits pending on both sides of the ocean and were making such stiff demands for royalties on exhibition flights in America that European aviators threatened to boycott the meet. The promoters finally satisfied the brothers with payment of $20,000, and the show went on.

Then more controversy erupted over the planned route for the renewal of the Gordon Bennett Cup race—twenty laps around a very tight 5-kilometer course lined with trees, buildings, and telegraph poles. One corner, dubbed *Dead Man's Turn*, offered only 100 feet of clearance to fly between pylon and the grandstand. One European pilot called the course suicide, causing four Frenchmen to stay out of the early events in protest.

Englishman Grahame-White, with his fastest Bleriot yet built, appeared to be the favorite to win, but his American rivals, aching to make up for being outshown at the recent Boston meet, also came well-prepared. The Wrights brought several planes, including their *Baby Grand* which featured a 60-hp V-8 engine, twice as powerful as any previous Wright machine. After Orville Wright made a trial run at 70 mph, the odds changed in his favor to win the speed contests.

Hamilton's 1910 flight at Seattle

Glenn Curtiss came to defend his title from the previous year, but after uncrating his first monoplane and surveying the competition, he decided against it. But there were more than enough entries—27 in all—to fill the gap left by him. Among the Americans were Charlie Hamilton, now flying his own biplane, John Moisant, piloting his own Bleroit, and the entire Wright exhibition team.

The meet began in a downpour, and a handful of aviators who braved the weather on the first day listened helplessly as their engines coughed, sputtered, and died with drowned ignitions. Grahame-White seemed to be more experienced, since he draped a blanket over his engine and put a heater under it. With little trouble he was the first in the air.

On subsequent days, as the weather improved, planes took to the sky with enough frequency to keep the spectators on edge. Charlie Hamilton's trick landings were especially amazing, and never failed to bring screams of terror from the crowds. He would climb to an altitude of a couple hundred feet, point the nose of his ship down, and then dive right for the crowd. At about five feet from the ground he would straighten up, and stop on a line right in front of the grandstand. No one could match that for thrills!

The stars of the Wright team were Arch Hoxsey and Ralph Johnstone. In one air show after another, they made headlines by chasing each other around the sky—they were the hottest ones on the team. Too hot, in fact, for Wilbur, for he was on them repeatedly for their recklessness. But their most memorable performance at Belmont was completely unplanned. One afternoon the two were dueling for an altitude record and they found themselves in high winds that increased until they were actually being blown backward. Johnstone calculated his airspeed at 40 mph against a wind of 80 mph, and he ended up 55 miles from the park before he could land in a clearing and tie his plane up before it blew away. Hoxsey had a similar wild ride and landed 25 miles away. Neither one ever approached an altitude record, but that was to be the first, and perhaps last, backward cross-country race in history.

Saturday, the 29th of October was a day for excitement, for this was the day on which the world's most advanced aircraft would be driven to their limits to win the Gordon Bennett Trophy and a $5,000 purse that went with it. A few minutes after the official start of the race at 8:30 A.M., Graham-White had his powerful 100-hp Bleroit airborne and racing around the course. Close behind was Frenchman Alfred Le Blanc in another Bleriot. At the 17th lap, Grahame-White's engine overheated, scorching his plane's fuselage. Smoke seared his throat and impaired his vision, but he was still able to complete the remaining three laps just as Le Blanc, running out of gas, went down on the backstretch, hanging up on one of the telegraph poles he had complained about.

Walter Brookings, chief pilot of the Wright team, was preparing to take off in the *Baby Grand* just as Le Blanc crashed, so he flew over to have a look. Pushed by a hefty tail wind and flying at 100 mph, he promptly lost control of his plane when a connecting rod broke. The undercarriage crumpled and the craft began to cartweel. After about the third somersault, Brookings was able to get off, but what was left of the machine continued to roll out of control. Luckily, neither pilot was seriously hurt, but with both planes out of the race, Grahame-White's time of 61 minutes and 4.74 seconds for the 100 kilometer distance stood untouched. Only three other pilots even finished the course, and John Moisant, who came in second, required almost an hour longer, including 38 minutes on the ground for repairs.

The final event of the meet—a 33-mile race across the crowded city, then out over New York Harbor, around the Statue of Liberty, and back—provided a new cause for protest and ill will. Originally, the race was open only to pilots who, during the meet, had completed a flight lasting at least an hour. But when it became apparent that very few aviators besides Grahame-White would meet that requirement, the judges abolished it, opening the race to everyone. Incensed, Grahame-White lodged a complaint, and when the judges ignored him, he considered withdrawing from the contest.

Even the rule change failed to produce a sporting contest. The race was scheduled for a Sunday; the devout Wright brothers never flew on the Sabbath, and neither did their team. John Moisant was scratched early on when he wrecked his Bleriot in a runway collision with Clifford Harmon's clumsy Farman. Only Count Jacques de Lesseps remained, that is until Grahame-White, figuring it was no contest, decided to stay in the race.

De Lesseps took off in his Bleriot first, but Grahame-White soon passed him and held a 65-second lead by the time he reached the balloon tethered over the Statue of Liberty, marking the turn. As shrill whistles from the boats filled the air, Grahame-White banked around the statue, headed across Brooklyn, and landed. He was being paraded around the race track wrapped in a Union Jack when it was announced that the competition was not yet over; John Moisant had appeared at the starting line with a new Bleriot. It was 4:06 P.M.—21 minutes after the official closing time for the race. The judges again had bent the rules, still hoping that an American would win.

Moisant, after mangling his own machine in the collision, had refused to call it quits. He and his brother had spotted a spare Bleriot in the injured Le Blanc's hangar and impulsively decided to buy it. While John supervised a quick switch of identification numbers on the plane's wing and tail, his brother Alfred was on the telephone to Le Blanc in his Manhattan hotel room to negotiate the purchase.

Le Blanc recovered sufficiently from his injuries to find a car and drive to Belmont Park. A haggle ensued over the price, so Alfred, growing impatient, offered $10,000, far more than the plane was worth, and Le Blanc readily accepted.

Within 10 minutes, with the painted numbers still wet, John Moisant taxied to the starting line and took off. As the Bleriot disappeared in the distance the crowd buzzed with anticipation. An American still had a chance for the prize.

In less than half an hour the lone aeroplane appeared again and landed amid the roar of the crowd. The judges deliberated, then made their announcement. By 43 seconds, John Moisant was the winner. The race was tainted, but the crowd went wild. Moisant was paraded in triumph around the field with an American flag draped over his shoulders.

Grahame-White was furious. Demanding a rerun, he cabled a protest to the Federation Aeronautique Internationale in Paris and then offered to race Moisant anywhere for a stake of $10,000. Moisant refused, figuring: "why risk my neck to beat him again?"

It was more than a year before the dispute was settled. The F.A.I. finally reversed the decision, and at an Aero Club dinner in New York in 1912, Grahame-White finally collected his $10,000 check—plus $500 accrued interest.

By then the aviation world had greatly changed. Ralph Johnstone had died less than three weeks after the Belmont meet. He was attempting to give spectators at Denver's Overland Park an extra thrill with his most daring feat, the spiral glide. Without warning, the tips of both wings folded up. Johnstone rode the crippled plane down from 800 feet, pulling at the warping wires all the way in a futile effort to right the ship.

John Moisant was also dead, killed in New Orleans on December 31, 1910, while stretching for a victory in Michelin's $4,000 contest for the longest sustained flight. His Bleriot went into a nose dive, apparently after the heavy gasoline load shifted foreward; however, no one ever knew for sure what caused the accident.

Arch Hoxsey was killed the same day in Los Angeles while trying to beat his own world's altitude record of 11,474 feet. He flew for an hour and a half to reach 7,000 feet, then suddenly started down in a spiral descent. As the little speck gradually grew larger it could be seen that the daredevil birdman and machine were rushing earthward in one perpendicular swirl after another. He seemed to gain control about 500 feet up, but after making a wide turn, the craft almost stood on end and a gust of wind hit, instantly turning the craft over.....the cracking of the spars and ripping of the cloth could be heard as the machine, a shapeless mass, hurtled to earth in a series of somersaults. Attendents rushed to the crumpled heap on the ground. The crowd grew silent and waited until the announcer megaphoned the fatal news, and then they turned homeward. All flying was over for the day, closing out a most tragic year in which so many lives of well-known pilots were lost.

Ralph Johnstone

John Moisant

Arch Hoxsey

Flight of the Vin Fiz

The year of 1911 proved to be a hallmark for aviation in America. In August, a wild exhibition of aerial display at the International Air Meet in Chicago saw one world record set, two pilots killed, and nine days of crowd-pleasing flying by a galaxy of the world's best airmen. The star of the meet was Lincoln Beachey, a flying madman who coaxed his Curtiss pusher to an altitude record of 11,642 feet, then, Harry Atwood, a Wright-trained pilot, stopped off while enroute from St. Louis to New York on a record-breaking cross country trip. But the surprise of the celebration was Calbraith Perry Rodgers, an unknown novice who captured the grand prize by staying airborne longer than anyone else—accumulating more than twenty-four hours in flight. When this was announced, the crowd was astonished, and many were heard to ask, "Who is this fellow Rodgers?"

Cal Rodgers was a jovial, nearly deaf giant of a man who would have upheld a family tradition of a naval career had not a childhood attack of scarlet fever severly impaired his hearing. Unable to get into Annapolis, he enrolled at Columbia University, where he played football and raced yachts and cars before taking up flying. At the Wright school in 1911 he soloed after only 90 minutes of instruction, a school record.

After winning the $11,285 prize at Chicago, he set his sights on a transcontinental pilgrimage. In 1910, newspaper publisher William Randolph Hearst announced a contest with a $50,000 prize for the first aerial coast-to-coast crossing of the United States within a 30-day period—the offer to expire on October 10, 1911. Not until a month before the deadline did anyone take off in pursuit of the prize, but Harry Atwood's distance record in August renewed interest in the contest. By the end of the first week in September, eight pilots had formally entered the race for the prize, but most never left the ground. The only real contenders were Robert Fowler, an outstanding graduate of the Wright School, James Ward, a former jockey with a Curtiss biplane, and Cal Rodgers.

Fowler was the first of the three to get underway. On September 11th he took off from San Francisco's Golden Gate Park and flew 129 miles east to the Sierra Nevadas. While attempting to cross Donner Pass, his rudder-control cable snapped, causing a crash in the trees. Fowler was not seriously injured, but his plane had to be rebuilt completely before he could take to the air again. Meanwhile, Jimmy Ward readied his Curtiss biplane for a September 13th lift-off from New York's Governor's Island. After a good start, he almost immediately found himself off-course, so far in fact, that he was completely lost.

The same day Cal Rodgers loaded a new custom-made Wright racing plane aboard a train in Dayton, Ohio and departed for New York. The new Wright biplane, known as Model EX, was slightly smaller than their Model B. It had a four-cylinder, 35-hp water-cooled engine which gave the plane a top speed of 55 miles an hour. Though the EX was the latest thing from the Wright factory, its control system was still rather primitive. The left-hand lever made the aircraft climb or descend by flexing a big elevator in the tail. A similar lever on the right warped the wings and caused the craft to bank. A hand lever at the top of the right stick controlled the rudder. There was no windshield, and the single seat was hard—the EX was said to be a sweet plane to fly, but terribly uncomfortable and physically exhausting.

But, at six-feet four-inches tall and weighing close to two hundred pounds, Rodgers looked like he could take the punishment. He was a handsome, shy individual who confidently had convinced the Armour Company of Chicago to back him financially if he would advertise *Vin Fiz*, a new grape soft drink that the meat packers were promoting. Armour agreed to pay Cal five dollars for every mile flown with the *Vin Fiz* advertisement lettered on the wings and tail of his plane. The company also arranged and paid for a special three-car train to follow Cal all the way to California.

On Sunday, September 17th, Cal's wife christened the plane with a bottle of *Vin Fiz* soda, Cal lit his trusty cigar, and he was off with a flourish—starting "...the most daring and spectacular feat of aviation that this country or even the world has ever known," as one newspaper reported.

After leaving the track at Sheepheads Bay, Cal circled Coney Island to drop *Vin Fiz* advertising flyers. Then he thrilled the crowds by skimming over Brooklyn, crossing the East River, and passing over the heart of Manhattan. Thousands of onlookers witnessed this most inspiring sight as Cal sailed directly over the city, heading west toward New Jersey to meet up with the special train which was waiting on the Erie Railroad tracks ready for the trip north to Middleton, New York, the first scheduled stop on the cross-country flight. The train consisted of an engine and three cars: a white 'hangar' car which was emblazoned with the *Vin Fiz* advertisements and which carried a backup plane, an automobile, spare parts, supplies, and baggage; a day coach which was used as an observer car; and a buffet-Pullman car in which Cal, his wife Mabel, his mother, and the Wright Company's chief mechanic, Charles Taylor, and other members of the party lived for the next few weeks.

It was quite a sight at the Middleton fairgrounds. Some five hundred autos were parked in a circle and a crowd of nine thousand people awaited Cal and the *Vin Fiz*. His first descent and landing were so easy that he didn't even lose the ashes from his cigar. All and all it had been a most satisfying day for the pilot and his biplane. Cal had left Sheepshead Bay around 4:30 P.M. and had covered 84 miles to Middleton in 105 minutes. After landing he remarked. "It's Chicago in four days if everything goes right."

Actually, things didn't continue going right. Trouble began the very next morning during takeoff. The plane's undercarriage struck a willow tree at the end of the field. The plane faltered, then recovered momentarily, but Cal could see that he was too low to clear a powerline, so he cut the engine. The plane hit another tree, tipped over and plummeted into a chicken coop. Without any safety strap, Cal landed on his feet in a tangle of wire, wood, fabric, and feathers. Somehow he managed to hang on to his cigar he had lit just before takeoff, but the plane was demolished. Under Charlie Taylor's direction, Cal's mechanics worked around the clock and put the plane back together in forty hours.

While Cal was stuck in Middleton, Fowler was still held up in California, and Ward was having engine trouble. Cal's planned four days to Chicago turned out to be twenty-one. His trip was plagued by blown spark plugs, broken landing skids, ignition troubles, and more crashes. After a forced landing on a farm in the Allegany Indian Reservation near Salamanc, he tried returning to the air only to pile into a barbed-wire fence. The *Vin Fiz* was demolished for the second time.

On September 27th the weather took a turn for the worse, causing more delays and treacherous flying in and around storm clouds. After surviving a hail storm, he flew over a low cloud cover which cut his visibility of the ground below, but he finally sailed into clear air and continued on to Huntington, Indiana where he met his train and called it a day. The next morning, on October 2nd, the weather was clear but gusty. To avoid bucking the gusts, Cal tried taking off downwind, but couldn't gain altitude. The *Vin Fiz* hopped and skipped across the field, heading toward a group of spectators. Rather than plow into the crowd, Cal swerved his plane to the right, still desperately trying to become airborne. The plane passed between two trees and under some telegraph wires. The left wing snagged on a small rise, the plane crumpled, and Cal was thrown clear. He wasn't injured, but his machine was smashed for the third time.

It was Sunday, October 8th, before Cal reached Chicago. He had come little more than 1,000 miles in three weeks, and it was obviously impossible to reach California before the October 10th deadline for the Hearst prize. Prize or no prize, he was determined to cross the continent simply to be the first to cross in an aeroplane.

To prove his resolution, he left Chicago the same day and headed southwest to Springfield, then on to Kansas City where a crowd of ten thousand welcomed him. Bad weather grounded him for a couple of days which gave the crew some time to work on the spark plug problem. As soon as the skies cleared, he was on his way again over Kansas and

Oklahoma, then on to Fort Worth, Texas. On October 18th he reached Dallas and sailed down the infield of the State Fair race track at 1:50 P.M. to the tumultuous applause of seventy-five thousand onlookers. After a fifteen-minute flight that thrilled the crowd, he headed westward to continue his long journey to the Pacific Coast.

The next day a piston crystallized, forcing the *Vin Fiz* down near Kyle. Charlie Taylor replaced the engine with a spare one from the train. More time was lost due to high winds so Cal took advantage of the delay and got some much needed rest in San Antonio.

On the 24th, he took off to pick up the Southern Pacific tracks, and flew 132 miles to Spofford, Texas. While attempting a take off the next morning, a propellor struck the ground. The plane swerved out of control and spun to the left, splintering both props, demolishing the undercarriage, and crumpling the wings.

By this time the crew had become quite proficient at repair, and the plane was ready to go the next morning. The rest of the trip across Texas was interrupted by high winds and smashed skids. On November 1st, Cal flew into Tucson, Arizona where he met briefly with Robert Fowler, who was still pushing eastward toward Florida.

After leaving Tucson, Cal went on to Mariposa, past Phoenix, then was forced down with no fuel at the Storal railroad siding. The next morning he flew on into California and as he approached the Salton Sea, the number-one cylinder in his engine exploded, showering his right arm with metal shards. In spite of a near calamity, he glided down for a perfect landing next to the Southern Pacific station at Imperial. The explosion wrecked the engine; Charlie Taylor had no choice but to replace it with the one which had been removed in Kyle, Texas. Meanwhile, a doctor worked on Cal for two hours to remove the engine fragments from his arm.

Cal set out again on the 4th and got as far as Banning. His spark plugs had loosened, and the radiator sprung a leak. The old troubles were plaguing him again.

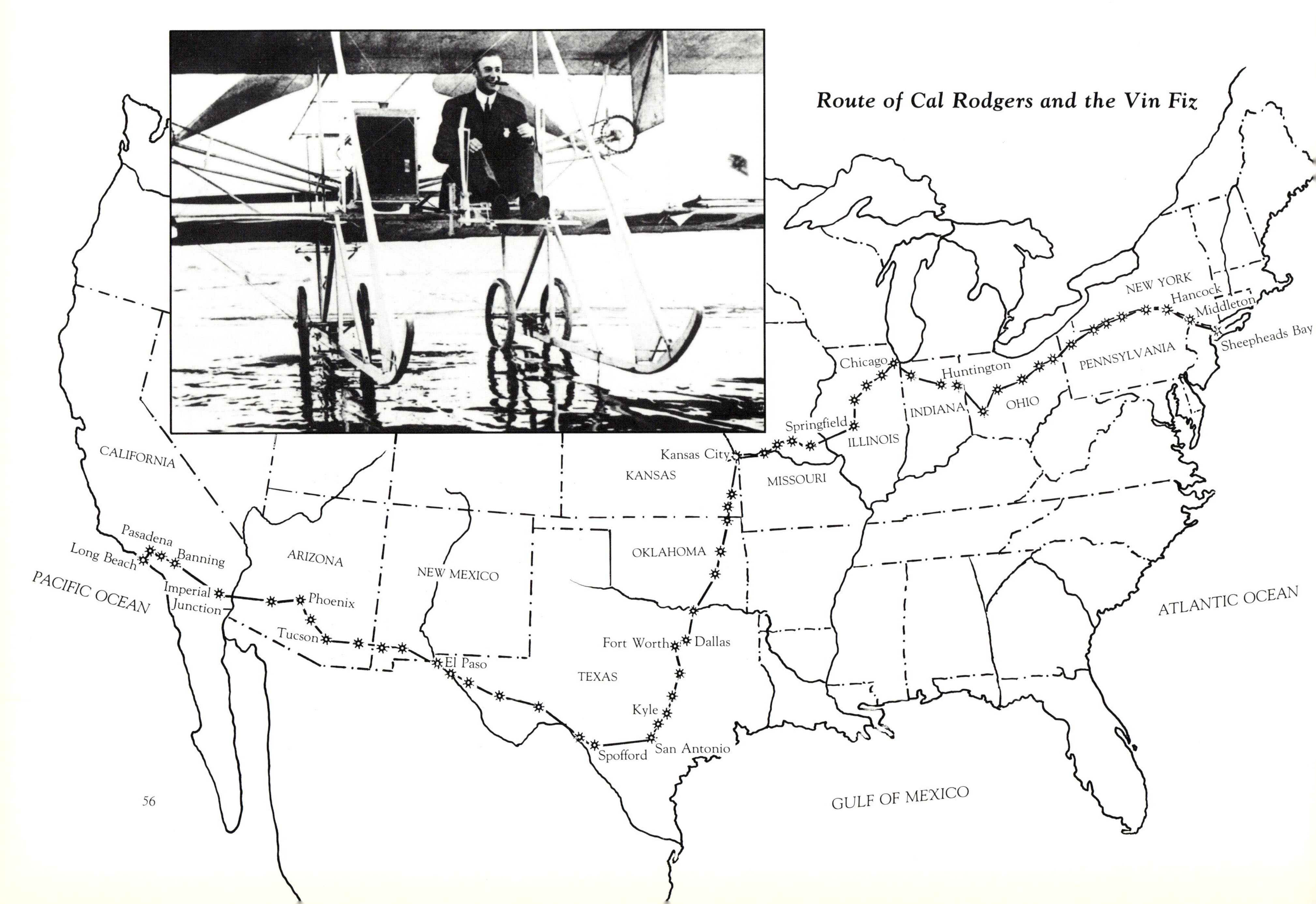
Route of Cal Rodgers and the Vin Fiz
PACIFIC OCEAN
CALIFORNIA
Pasadena
Long Beach
Banning
Imperial
Junction
ARIZONA
Phoenix
Tucson
NEW MEXICO
El Paso
TEXAS
Fort Worth
Dallas
Kyle
Spofford
San Antonio
KANSAS
Kansas City
OKLAHOMA
MISSOURI
Springfield
ILLINOIS
Chicago
INDIANA
Huntington
OHIO
PENNSYLVANIA
NEW YORK
Hancock
Middleton
Sheepheads Bay
ATLANTIC OCEAN
GULF OF MEXICO

The next day, with only 75 miles to go before reaching his official destination, Cal left Banning, but was soon forced down with a broken gas line. He finally reached Pasadena at 4:08 on the afternoon of November 5th. This was the forty-ninth day since leaving New York, and he had covered 4,231 railroad miles, with 86 stops along the way.

Cal landed at Tournament Park and was mobbed by ten thousand wildly cheering people who rushed onto the field and swarmed his plane before police could rescue him. Wrapped in an American flag, Cal was driven around the field, then taken to the Hotel Maryland, where he celebrated by drinking a glass of milk and eating some crackers. At that point Cal didn't see much romance in flying, and was glad the trip was over. But he was pleased to be the one to have made it, though his opinion was that his record would not last for long. He felt that the flight could easily be made in thirty days or less.

Despite the sense of finality to his arrival in Pasadena, Cal did not consider his journey over until he reached the Pacific Ocean. On Sunday, November 12th, he left Pasadena and headed for Long Beach. Halfway there he crashed in a plowed field while attempting an emergency landing. For the fifth time, the *Vin Fiz* was demolished. Cal was hauled from the wreckage bruised and unconcious, and didn't awaken until the next day in the hospital. His ankle was broken, but he was in good spirits, sitting up in bed, smoking a cigar and visiting with family and friends.

It was almost a month before he was well enough to be up and around again. On Sunday, December 10th, he hobbled out to his plane, tucked his crutches beside him, and took off to finish his flight. Landing in the sand at Long Beach, he wet his wheels in the surf as a massive crowd of fifty thousand people cheered from the boardwalk. After eighty-four days, five major crashes, numerous lesser mishaps on takeoff or landing, engine failures in mid-air, and a hospital stay, America had been crossed by air. Cal Rodger's odyssey was finally over.

The Stunt of Stunts

Silas Christofferson was a mechanical genius; he wasn't content to sit behind a drafting table, or slave in the Bennett Motor Company shop in Portland, Oregon till his dying day. Speed and thrills were more his style, and from the time in 1908 when he began building a flying machine, he was out to put some excitement into his life. On Sundays, Si raced cars at the Rose City track; during off hours he worked on his aeroplanes, and whenever he had the chance, he thrilled the Portlanders with his his flying boat, galloping down the Willamette River playing leap frog under one bridge and over the next, all the way through the heart of the city. Then, to really get the attention of the onlookers, he would perform a series of death dives. Climbing a mile above the city center, he would dive straight down, then pull out 75 feet above the ground. His philosophy was that "no stunt was dangerous if he got back alive."

Si was known all over the Northwest for his daredevil flights, but his ultimate stunt was planned for execution during the Rose City Festival of 1912. Weeks were spent designing and preparing for his surprise performance.

On the 11th of June, he and his crew made last minute preparations as crowds of Festival-goers filled the streets and buildings of downtown Portland. Just before the grand parade, as thousands of onlookers lined the streets and rooftops, Si poured the gas to his 40-hp engine and sped his box kite machine across the roof of the Multnomah Hotel, up his man-made ramp, and into the air to slip between the buildings, and soar over the rooftops. Twelve minutes later he landed safely in a field across the Columbia River. This day would be remembered by thousands of Portlanders and Rose Festival visitors, for Si's flight from the Multnomah was the stunt of all stunts, never to be done again.

Racing the Dirt Tracks

By 1915 speed was on everyone's mind. Agencies around the country were offering automobiles as a replacement for four-legged hayburners, and livery stables were feeling hot competition from the gas guzzlers. People galore could hardly wait to don a duster and goggles for their first ride in a horseless carriage. And it was only natural that some were not content with only a ride but would want to see how fast they could go. Of all the speedsters, Barney Oldfield was king. He was the first man to race a motorcar at a mile a minute, and had recently set a record of 111.5 miles per hour in his 300-horsepower Christie in Chicago. Word had gotten around Boise, Idaho that Oldfield was on his last tour before retirement from the dirt track and there might be a chance that he could appear in town. It was a promoter's dream, for not only could they get Barney Oldfield, but also another attraction—DeLloyd Thompson, pilot extraordinaire who had just set a record by looping-the-loop 53 consecutive times. Plus, he was sure to perform his tumble flight, better known as the *Undertaker's Drop*, in which he and his plane fell end over end for several thousand feet before pulling out close to the ground.

A performance was planned for June 24th, and handbills plastered the town to bring out the crowd. The billing was emblazoned with glowing phrases of how Thompson not only would cut capers in the air, but also race his plane against the invincible Oldfield. A press agent expounded that the program might be too strong for the weak-hearted, writing that "...people had been known to faint from the shock of watching Oldfield and Thompson taunt the Grim Reaper."

He suggested that persons of delicate constitution stay away from the fairgounds. However, if they must go, the Chief of Police had made arrangements for ambulances, trained nurses, and a platoon of Red Cross volunteers to minister to any and all casualties: "Things will be reasonably safe at the show, and there won't be anything that the coroner can not handle."

The warning to stay away was so strong that nobody wanted to go except citizens between the ages of three and ninety-five. Mayor Jeremiah Robinson declared a half-day holiday in the city. Stores promptly closed at 2:30 in the afternoon, and the citizens of Boise rushed to the fairgrounds.

A light breeze was blowing, and the weather was fair and warm—a perfect day for the performance. Streetcars delivered at least 3,500 spectators to the track, and about 700 autos were parked on the grounds. Hundreds who were not convinced that the motor car was reliable arrived by horse and buggy. Boise society jammed the box seats, and the others crammed the grandstands. The crowd spilled outside the track, and a few spectators manned haystacks in the adjoining fields for a cheap seat to the show.

Barney Oldfield, chomping his usual cigar, warmed up the incoming crowd by roaring past the grandstand. The master of ceremonies asked him to wait until the rest of the crowd was in so all could see. Oldfield briefly idled the engine of his 100-horsepower Fiat Cyclone, then roared down the course and around the first turn. On the backstretch he let in even more gas and the white streak of motorcar looked like a hawk in hot pursuit of its prey. He skidded around the final turn and roared down the homestretch to the acclaim of thousands. His time for the mile was 48 seconds, not up to the Chicago mark, but the best that Boise had ever seen. Oldfield said, "If the track had been in better shape I could have done better."

Then it was time for a change of pace and Thompson started the engine of his aeroplane, then checked his gauges and controls to make sure everything was in good order. Just a few weeks before, an embarrassing thing had happened while he was looping-the-loop. A wheel fell off and struck him in the face. Dazed but not daunted, he hurled the wheel from the cockpit, completed his routine, and landed without mishap. Nothing of the sort, he hoped, would mar the flight this day.

After ascending to about 400 feet he began to loop. Everything held together as he continued one loop after another. Roars of approval rose from the ground as he completed a few dozen more and headed back to earth.

Without interruption, Oldfield made his second assault on the speed record. Seated in a 300-horsepower Christie, and chewing a fresh cigar, he roared around the track, but the best he could do was 48 seconds, the same time as his first attempt.

The afternoon was climaxed with the promised race of the day—Thompson and Oldfield were to battle twice around the oval track. Thompson lost no time in getting into the air and made a circle to align with Oldfield for an even start in front of the grandstand. Around the track they raced, jockeying for position. The wheels of Thompson's plane were almost on Barney's helmet much of the way, with the wind from the propeller kindling his cigar to a glowing torch. The spectators were on their feet in frenzied excitement. The second lap brought more anxiety, and Thompson finally edged his plane ahead in the home stretch. Then he soared up to mock attack the nearby fort. Shells from the ground burst around him, and the fort blew up with a blazing roar. It was an afternoon of excitement that the citizens of Boise would never forget for the rest of their lives.

Doing 'em One Better

Although Katharine Stinson was only fourteen years old she was determined about her future, dreaming of becoming an accomplished pianist. A major problem faced her though: she didn't have sufficient funds to continue her education in the music field.

After reading that aviators were earning substantial sums of money for exhibition flying, she decided to give it a go, figuring that anything a man could do she could do, maybe even better. She thought that if she worked really hard, after a few shows she should have enough money to be able to return to her music career.

Finding an aviation school in which to learn was not an easy task, as many were going out of business, but Katharine finally settled on Max Lillie's spring class at Circero Field in Chicago. Right from the start she demonstrated a great deal of natural talent and soloed after a few lessons in a Wright B Flyer, at age sixteen becoming the fourth and youngest woman in America to earn her pilot's license. Since she was so young, she didn't start on the exhibition circuit immediately but continued to practice flying, loving it so much that all her dreams of music were soon abandoned.

An exhibition flight in Cincinnati, Ohio in July of 1913 was the beginning of an aviation career that took her to meets all around the country. It wasn't long before she was widely recognized and in demand both within and outside of aviation circles. She was the first woman authorized to fly the airmail, carrying 1,333 postcards and letters in four days from the fairgrounds to the Federal Building in downtown Helena, Montana. Then she was asked to participate in the 1913 Rose Parade in Pasadena, California. With her aircraft decoratively covered with roses, she flew the entire length of the parade, to the approval of all in view.

On July 18, 1915, at Cicero Field in Chicago, Katharine became the first woman in the world to loop-the-loop. Expanding on this feat, she developed her Dippytwist loop—a vertical bank in which the aircraft rolled wing-over-wing when the top of the loop was reached. Performing this maneuver for the first time on November 21st, she followed it in her next flight with a routine of eight consecutive loops, thirty seconds of upside down flying, and finishing up with a series of spiral spins.

Of all her exhibition flights, perhaps the most spectacular was held on December 17th. After hearing that stunter Art Smith had looped-the-loop at night, leaving behind him a trail of fire, Katharine was determined to outdo him. Attaching magnesium flares to her aircraft, she took to the air over Los Angeles. It wasn't long before the darkness was broken as she traced the letters 'CAL' in the nighttime sky. Then she looped-the-loop, flew upside down, and dropped in a spiral to within one hundred feet of the ground, trailing a shower of sparks all the way. It was a magnificient piece of flying, and a spectacle that few would forget. There was little question that the male of the species had been done one better that night in the December sky.

The Ultimate Exhibition Flyer

Lincoln Beachey believed he was born to fly. By 1910, at the age of 23, he had built and operated his own dirigible, and although he had never flown a fixed-wing aircraft he felt fully qualified. After hanging around the Curtiss exhibition team, working as a mechanic and bumming rides whenever he could, he offered his services to Curtiss as an exhibition pilot. Curtiss somehow sensed that the brash young dirigible pilot had the makings of a good flier so he let him try in spite of the fact that Beachey refused any instruction. Once he was in the air he did well, demonstrating an uncanny ablility to fly and maneuver the rather primitive flying machine, but he seemed unable to land it without smashing it up. Curtiss must have had a great deal of patience, because he continued to allow Beachey to take off and crash until he finally got the hang of landing well enough to gain a spot on the exhibition team tour of the East Coast in 1911.

Beachey rapidly developed a very distinctive style of flying which electrified the crowds that gathered for the show. In marked contrast to other pilots, Beachey never seemed to fly straight and level, but was always twisting and turning, and bucking up and down. He usually concluded his act by climbing to about 5,000 feet, then pushing the rickety Curtiss biplane over into a vertical dive, heading straight for the ground. With fabric rippling and guy wires whining, he held the speedy descent until it seemed that a crash was inevitable. Then, at the last moment, he pulled out, not far over the heads of the spectators, and touched down right in front of the grandstand.

When it came to flying in and out of tight places, there was no other pilot who could approach Beachey's skill and precision. One of his most famous tight-squeeze flights took place in June of 1911. Flying out of Buffalo, New York he announced his intention to fly over Niagara Falls.

Taking off in a light rain, he climbed to around 2,000 feet, then came roaring down the river to the brink of the falls. Twice he circled low to give the crowd of 15,000 an extra thrill before plunging into the gorge below. Dripping wet, he emerged safely from the mist at the foot of the cascading water, only to get blasted by the wash from the power tunnel outlet which shot out from the rocky precipice. He recovered barely in time to make the pass under the bridge 400 yards downstream from the base of the falls. The space he flew through was 168 feet high and barely 100 feet from side to side. When almost in the spray of the whirlpool rapids, he pointed toward the cliffs on the Canadian side, pulled up to barely squeak over the edge of the gorge and plunked down onto firm ground.

It was easy enough to go over the falls, but climbing back out of the gorge was another matter.

As exhibition flying was becoming more commonplace, people were coming to expect more and more dangerous stunts, and Beachey was one of the best to satisfy their lust. He probably flew more exhibition dates in 1911 and 1912 than any other pilot in America. But many of the pilots were getting killed by pushing themselves and their machines beyond safe limits in an attempt to put on a good show, and Beachey began to be blamed for many of the fatalities. It got so bad that some newspapers referred to fatal accidents as '*pulling a Beachey*'—and this bothered him terribly. He also began to believe that the public only wanted to see him kill himself, so he decided it was time to quit.

For awhile he went into vaudeville, but it was a dismal act. Then, one day he heard about a fellow in France looping the loop. Nobody had ever done that before. Now Beachey's reputation was at stake. He got Curtiss to build him a specially braced plane that could withstand the maneuvers he contemplated. After some testing, redesigning, and complete rebuilding, he was ready to try it out. His first attempt was so easy that he did three more loops in succession over the Polo Grounds at Coronado, California on November 15, 1913.

The pressure to top himself became relentless. He made a quick trip to France and bought two 80-horsepower Gnome rotary engines which promised to keep running better when flying upside down. Meanwhile, his mechanics were at work building a new biplane they called the *Little Looper*, which was probably the finest aircraft built in America at that time. Beachey had no difficulty maintaining control upside down, right side up, slow or fast—the *Little Looper* could hit speeds up to 85 miles per hour and climb at an impressive rate of 1,125 feet per minute. After a little practice, he developed a new maneuver for his bag of tricks—a vertical-S combination of outside and inside loops.

The 1914 season was Beachey's busiest and most successful. By the end of the year it was estimated that he had looped 1,000 times before seventeen million people in 126 cities. His fee was $500 for the first loop at an exhibition plus $200 for each loop after that.

His terms were cash in advance, and it was not unusual for him to earn up to $1,500 for a six-loop day's work.

As the year wore on, the news of war in Europe captured the headlines. There were fewer and fewer reports of Beachey's accomplishments. The threat of war was bringing the carefree days of aviation to an end. But for Lincoln Beachey, there was still time for one more fling. The Panama-Pacific International Exposition, scheduled to be held in San Francisco, seemed like a good opportunity to grab some headlines again. He ordered a radically different new plane for the stunts at the exposition. Though he had flown it a few times he didn't take it to the show, but relied upon the *Little Looper* for the opening performance on February 21, 1915.

Fair officials talked Beachey into exhibiting his new monoplane, so he unveiled it at the fairgrounds on March 13th, looping three times for the spectators before rain called a halt to the day's flying.

The next day was a Sunday, and a crowd of fifty thousand lined the field to see the monoplane take off with the renowned Beachey at the controls.

That afternoon he climbed into his machine and ascended a mile high so that all could see. He started with several graceful, effortless-looking loops, then he began his vertical-S maneuvers. The plane's behavior in the top half of the S was normal, but when he pulled back into the bottom half, the monoplane went into a screaming, uncontrolled dive in which it hit speeds in excess of over 200 miles per hour. As Beachey tried to pull out of the dive, there was a loud, sickening crack as first the left and then the right wing snapped and folded upward around the body of the plane. The machine plunged headlong and hit the bay with a big splash and sank out of sight.

The Flying Fool had made his last flight. The greatest of the early exhibition fliers had paid the ultimate price, and his death climaxed an era that brought aerial excitement to vast audiences of thrill seekers around the nation.

Chapter

4

Wings to War

Wally Olson piloting his Curtiss Jenny at Vancouver

Up until World War I the U.S. Government felt little need to invest much in military aviation, though it did form an Aeronautical Division of the Signal Corps in July of 1907 to investigate what was going on across the Atlantic. Evidently the aerial activity in Europe spurred them to action, for on December 23, 1907, the Signal Corps advertised for an airplane—a machine which could carry a pilot and passenger, be capable of staying in the air one hour without landing, carry enough fuel for a flight of 125 miles, and be able to average 40 miles an hour over a ten-mile course. As soon as the bid was let, the press began to editorialize: "...Surely someone in the Signal Corps was suffering from grand delusions—a military airship that would fill that criterion had not yet been invented, and what folly it was to waste large sums of money on pipedreams."

The Wright brothers did not share in the skepticism, for they had practically written the specifications. It was four years since their first successful flight at Kitty Hawk, and up until this time they and their accomplishments had not been recognized in America. Twice, they offered their machine to the War Department and twice they were turned down. However, the European powers gladly purchased and employed the Wright patents—not all countries were so blind to the possibilities of such a marvelous invention in time of warfare.

Since the Wright Flyer was the only machine that came close to fulfilling all of the specifications, the brothers received a contract in February of 1908 for delivering a finished plane in two hundred days. They lost no time in getting to work and modifiying their *Flyer* to be usable in a war effort. By that summer Wilbur had sailed for Europe to demonstrate their capabilities, while Orville prepared for the U.S. Army demonstrations—and on September 3rd people by the thousands gathered at Ft. Meyer, Virginia to see an aeroplane in flight for the first time. Orville thrilled the crowds with his flying, and the trials were proceeding perfectly, when suddenly tragedy struck. Lieutenant Thomas

Selfridge was riding as an observer with Orville, when, without a hint of warning, a propeller blade disintegrated which severed a bracing wire, causing the tail unit to collapse. For a brief period the craft kept its course, but suddenly fell, regained for a moment, and then crashed in a cloud of dust.

The rescue party found Orville hanging from the guy wires. Considering the severity of the crash, it was a wonder he wasn't killed, though he was in severe shock with four broken ribs, a fractured left leg and dislocated hip, plus fractures of his right hip bone. Lieutenant Selfridge was not so lucky. He had a fractured skull, and within a few hours he was dead—the first man in the world to lose his life in a powered aircraft accident.

In spite of the tragedy, Orville recovered to repair the ship and complete the trials the following summer, and on August 2nd of 1909, at the cost of $25,000, the United States of America purchased her first airplane.

But the government was slow in advancing aviation, and it was 1911 before its first flying school was established at College Park, Maryland. By the next year it had grown to fourteen flying officers, thirty-nine enlisted men, and nine airplanes of the Wright, Curtiss, and Burgess manufacture.

By 1913 most military operations had been shifted to San Diego, California where a new Signal Corps School was established. The fleet of aircraft had been up to twenty-eight, but nine had been written off in crashes, and eleven pilots had lost their lives. As a result, the pusher-type Wright and Curtiss aircraft were condemned, leaving the Army with only five air-worthy machines.

In the summer of 1914 Europe was at war; on July 18th Congress authorized the Aviation Section of the Signal Corps with a paper strength of sixty officers, two hundred sixty enlisted men, and six airplanes. President Woodrow Wilson, hoping to avoid the disastrous European conflict, enjoined the country to remain neutral, but many Americans thought Germany was wrong and found their way to the front to serve with the Allies.

American pilots flew in several squadrons, but the most renowned was the *Escadrille Americane*, which was organized in the spring of 1916 under the command of French officers. Within months of being sent to the Front, this small band of American volunteers, determined to pay their country's debt to France, had run up such a combat record that the German Ambassador lodged a formal complaint. German officials were outraged that American citizens were flying French aircraft and challenging the Germans in the sky when the United States was supposed to be neutral. Futhermore, it was pointed out that the aircraft bore the American flag insignia, and that the squadron designation actually included the name of America.

The Wilson government bowed to the German pressure, and ordered, through diplomatic channels, that the American volunteers could no longer operate under the *Escadrille Americane*. This was a blow to the group, for most of them felt that they would lose an important feature of their identity. To no avail, they argued that they should be able to continue to fight under their own colors so, using Yankee ingenuity, they substituted a name to pay honor to Marquis de Lafayette, the young Frenchman who volunteered to fight for the new world colonies. France couldn't be happier, taking the viewpoint that an American squadron serving in its air service had important political implications. Thus, the *Lafayette Escadrille* was born, and it wasn't long before the pilots saw action, and the *Escadrille* flew into romanticized immortality. Whenever one of the volunteers was promoted or received a decoration, the French made sure the news was spread around the world.

For the first time in history, battles were being won and lost depending on who had control of the air. When the war started, both sides initially used the airplane for observation of equipment movements and photographing enemy positions. The idea of combat in the air was only a myth, and hostile pilots often exchanged a wave of the hand in greeting as they continued on their mission. But it was inevitable that simple

observation would soon evolve into aerial skirmishes. At first revolvers and rifles were used in air-to-air combat. Then a military breakthrough developed with the French invention of a gun to shoot through the propellor. The Germans took up the idea and improved on it; suddenly, new technology took priority, and as soon as one side brought out a new or better development, the other side strove to equal or surpass it. Designers became almost as deeply immersed in battle as the pilots, and aerial combat changed by the week.

Air superiority meant victory, and all of the world powers were in a race to gain that control. When the United States entered the war in April of 1917, she was, with little doubt, a rank amateur. Since the Aviation Section of the U.S. Signal Corps was formed in 1907, the world had spent more than $100 million on aeronautics. Of that amount, the U.S. Congress had begrudgingly appropriated $435,000 to advance aviation in America, leaving the nation totally unprepared for modern warfare.

After America entered the conflict, the French Premier asked that a flying corps of 5,000 pilots, 50,000 mechanics, and 4,500 planes be sent to the Front for the spring campaign of 1918. In addition, he asked that American factories produce 2,000 planes and 4,000 engines every month. This appeal brought home to President Wilson's administration the pitiful situation that existed with the Allied forces.

At that time the American situation was even worse. The Aviation Section was composed of sixty-five officers and around a thousand enlisted men. There were fifty-five planes, but fifty-one were obsolete. Of the officers, only thirty-five were capable of active duty as aviators, and none had any experience with aircraft guns, bombs, or bombing devices—thus, the United States entered the war with five or six qualified military aviators who were without practical knowledge of aircraft armament, and who did not have a single plane fit for use! In an effort to overcome the past negligence, Congress began authorizing a huge amount of money for military aviation. In July of 1917 the sum of $640 million was appropriated for expanding the Air Service, and the Joint Army and Navy Technical Aircraft Board called for 8,075 training planes and 12,400 service planes—all to be produced within 12 months.

Few Americans realized that the General Staff knew practically nothing about military aeronautics. Not a single officer in Washington, D.C. had attended a flying school, or had any practical experience about the needs of the Air Service. To make matters worse, most of the upper echelon of officers were more concerned with military protocol than success in the air. At the outset, the General Staff required military aviators to wear boots *and spurs*! Six months later it authorized them to wear the insignia of wings but continued to require spurs with boots. After the United States had been at war for a year, the General Staff concluded that the aviators might safely be relieved of their spurs, expecially since their wings indicated that they rode airplanes rather than horses.

When America entered the war there were only two small flying fields, and no plans for training the thousands of aviators who would have to be sent to France. But the Americans rallied, and by the third week of May, schools of military aeronautics had been opened in eight universities and institutes of technology. There was no lack of volunteers, as air-struck youths with a sense of daring flocked to aviation training centers. Their applications poured into the War Department by the tens of thousands. Extra rank and pay might have been incentives, but to most volunteers, the prospect of novel and exciting adventures probably had more to do with the unexpected response. Aviators were the idols of the war. From the exploits of combat pilots in the skies over Europe, war correspondents had created the legend of a new elite, a modern chivalric order, the volunteers of the *Escadrille*. As the first Americans to become masters of aerial warfare, they helped to develop the flying and techniques which afterward had to be learned by the Air Service. Tales of the valor and victories of the volunteers in the *Lafayette Escadrille* ran through the press for a year before the country entered the war. The *cult of the ace* was taking precedence over all other news from the war front and Uncle Sam was luring young men into the air service. With colorful posters emblazoned: "Be an American Ace!", and government promises too good to be true, the thought of being one of the elite was just too great to pass up. Before it was over, 38,000 high-spirited youth volunteered for the Air Service. Of these, 23,000 entered flight school, and 10,000 came out as aviators, with an equal number as mechanics.

Patriotism wasn't limited only to the young men of the country. Many women who were experienced pilots tried to volunteer their services. Ruth Law pleaded with the War Department to be permitted to enlist and go to the front as an aviator, but she was flatly turned down. Eventually, the Treasury Department was glad to avail itself of her services, and clad in an honorary uniform, she flew around the country in behalf of Liberty Loan drives and later, Army recruiting. Katherine Stinson also tried to enlist in the Air Services, but she and her sister had to be satisfied with training pilots for the wartime effort. Other women were likewise turned down from active duty, as authorities in Washington became outraged at the very thought of women in battle.

Meanwhile, work began on the twenty-seven flying fields scheduled for training pilots around the country. When the small cadre of qualified instructors became overwhelmed with students, combat veterans were called from overseas to handle the overload. At first their attempts at teaching the realities of combat flying met with stiff criticism and anguished cries of showoff stunting. They often were threatened with court-martial, but soon the impact of techniques taught was too obvious to ignore. Airfields had the reputation of being aviator graveyards. Conventionally trained men continued to be killed in flight situations they couldn't handle. The mad rush to fulfill the enthusiastic Yankee boast of "darkening the skies of Germany with airplanes" produced appalling death rates among students and instructors alike. Stunting was a part of survival, and any pilot who didn't learn that wasn't going to survive long at the Front.

Additionally, the flying schools suffered from a lack of advanced training planes. The Germans were flying the Albatross and Fokker triplanes, France had the Nieuport and Spads, Great Britain the Sopwith Camel and the Bristow fighter. All that America had was the *Jenny*, a sports plane that Glenn Curtiss had modified with dual controls. The Curtiss JN-4 became the standard training plane, beloved by many who flew her, but hardly a competitor with the European warships.

The *Jenny* was very different from her European counterparts. All of the American pilots who trained in her may have been able to fly, but they were not nearly ready for combat. As it turned out, the airfield at Issoudun, France became not only an advanced, but also a primary, training school for the cadets to be retrained in at least six types of French aircraft before they could be assigned to active service.

From the beginning , the American pilots were under tremendous handicaps. The Nieuport planes assigned to them were obsolete, tricky to fly, and contained no armament whatsoever. The American authorities wouldn't even give the flyers a parachute, which was standard issue for all of the German aviators.

In spite of the handicaps, the Americans learned quickly under the command of their Air Service Officer, Colonel 'Billy' Mitchell.

So when the Allies set out to meet the Germans head-on at St. Mihiel in the fall of 1918, Colonel Mitchell's pilots were ready for the first mass air campaign in history. His deployment of 500 fighters and light bombers over the front lines, plus two waves of 500 planes each to attack the German supply depots, communication centers, and transportation routes, threw the German war machine into total disarray. In just a matter of months, the flyers of the Air Service became second to none in the world in aggressiveness and skill, and their actions did much to bring a rapid end to the war. During their relatively short time at the Front, American pilots had a confirmed score of downing 781 enemy planes, with losses of 289 of their own in air battles.

After the Armistice, Mitchell returned home a general, convinced that aviation had come of age and that the airplane had revolutionized warfare. As commander of the largest aerial fleet ever used in war, he resolved to awaken the nation to the need of establishing a well-organized air force, entirely independent of the Army and Navy, but he had a difficult time convincing the bureaucracy. The Army Reorganization Act of 1920 fell far short of granting aviators the independence they wanted, leaving tactical squadrons under the control of ground commanders who saw little value of the Air Service other than an extension of their communication system. It would be years before American military planners became wise enough, or were forced, to include airpower in their logistics.

Although the war was over, it was far from forgotten, and stories from the cadet camps to the front lines would live on to be told and retold for generations to come....

A Boyhood Charade

No sooner had the United States declared war against Germany than the town was emblazoned with posters: "Join Aviation—Fight the War with Wings!"

If you were between the ages of eighteen and thirty-five, all you had to do was sign up and you'd find yourself a flier for Uncle Sam. And Dean Smith got caught up in the fever.

Some of the university classmen of Principia Military School in St. Louis had already enrolled as cadets for training to become flying officers in the Air Service; Dean wanted badly to join them. But he knew he didn't stand a chance since two years of college were required to become a cadet, and he was just finishing his high school course. Even if he couldn't fly, he figured he would maybe be around planes if he enlisted, so he badgered his mother until she finally gave in, perhaps hoping that the fighting would be over before her son could be shipped overseas.

As Dean stepped into the recruiting office he had but one concern; it was still two months until his seventeenth birthday. His fear was groundless, for he simply wrote down a birth date two years earlier than was correct. The recruiting sergeant didn't pay much attention, as Dean's six-foot, four-inch height overshadowed his youthful looks. The physical examination didn't pose any problem either, since it seemed to consist solely of finding out if he had all his arms and legs and could stand without falling. Before he could draw a deep breath, he was a soldier.

After a long train ride to Texas, Dean got his first taste of Army life. As far as he could see there was flat, dry prairie lined with thousands of white tents. As everyone piled off the train he suddenly became part of the melee, standing in the hot sun wondering what would come next. After the typical Army wait, the mass was split into groups of 150 rookies each, and shortly a Lieutenant faced the bunch that Dean was with, and announced, "You are now in the 125th Aero Squadron. All men with previous military experience, one step foreward." There was no response. After a long wait, Dean spoke up, "I have been to military school, if that is any help to you."

This one act of speaking out earned him an instant position of drill sergeant, and the command to get the group organized. In future weeks he accustomed himself to the Army way, and before long finagled himself a permanent sergeant's warrant.

The outlook of being around airplanes was pretty grim at Kelly. There was only a small class being trained to become instructors, and all of the pupils had learned to fly as civilians. The fact was, at that time no one knew much about flying. In teaching, the blind led the blind; the only way anyone learned anything much more advanced than a gentle turn was by trial and error. By pulling on the controls this way and that, pilots gradually discovered what could and what could not be done. Those not killed in stalls and spins passed their knowledge of success onto others.

With his sergeant's position, Dean had more spare time and started haunting the flying areas every chance he could, nosing around and asking questions, trying to find out what it was all about. He discovered that a primary school was being prepared for the cadets that would soon be arriving from ground school. He started conniving: since he had enlisted in the Army and he was underage, and he had gotten sergeant's stripes with some bogus paperwork, why couldn't he try out for flying?

Dean's devil-may-care attitude gave him the courage to attempt a monumental piece of brass. With a sheet of parchment in hand, he went to work with pen and ink, then added ribbon and sealing wax for authority. The result was an imposing looking document, not worth a plug nickel, since he had signed it himself. Proud of his handiwork, he lost no time in presenting it to Joe-Ben Levry, the civilian head of the instructor's school.

Levry was one of the really hot acrobatic pilots of the day, and had nothing but contempt for smartalecks who thought they were pilots after a few lessons. He asked Dean how much flight training he'd had. Dean gulped, and said, "None, sir."

"Don't sir me. My name is Joe-Ben Levry—call me one or the other; I'm no damned officer. Glad for once to get someone who doesn't know about flying. Come on, I'll give you a ride."

And what a ride it was. Joe-Ben put the *Jenny* through a series of maneuvers until Dean couldn't tell one stunt from another, the way he was crammed into the cockpit. He was only semi-conscious when Joe-Ben finally leveled off and bore in for a landing.

When asked how he liked it, Dean lied through his teeth, "Fine, that was wonderful." He was deathly afraid that if he didn't put up a good front he would be considered unsuitable, and he wasn't about to admit the state he was actually in.

Joe-Ben didn't mess around. The flight had but one purpose—a test to see if Dean had any fear of flying or possibility to be a pilot. Dean's reaction seemed to be satisfactory, for he was turned over to Lt. 'Shorty' Hall to learn about the finer points of a *Jenny*, and to start flight training. It didn't take long to learn about the instruments; all a *Jenny* possessed was an engine tachometer, an altimeter, a thermometer for the engine coolant, oil pressure gauge, and a clock. After the brief orientation, the engine was started and Dean was off on his second trip into the air. This time the ride was smoother, and he even had a chance to handle the controls, but he became so engrossed in maneuvering the plane that he lost track of where they were, and Hall had to point the way back to the field.

After they were on the ground, Dean's head was still in the clouds. He was so overwhelmed by the fact that he was actually flying a plane, he had avoided the reality that he conned his way there. His dream bubble burst early the next morning when Hall greeted him with a curt, "Levry wants to see you in his office, immediately."

Joe-Ben wasted no time. "The officer in charge of flying was here yesterday, and saw your name, but it was not listed on the roster of student pilots. Who issued the orders assigning you here?"

Dean exclaimed, "Nobody. That is, that is, I did."

"Great God Almighty! *You* issued the orders! You, a miserable two-bit sergeant, are issuing flying orders. Just who do think you are?" For the next ten minutes he chewed Dean out without pause. Then he reiterated how serious the matter was; there could be a court-martial on six different counts, and he could spend the rest of his life in Leavenworth. He wound up by telling him he had made a full report to the commanding officer of the post. Then he calmed down and said, "When you get in front of the colonel, tell him you want to fly more than anything in the world. Tell him that is the only reason you tried this stunt. Tell him you believe you are qualified to become a pilot. Tell him your instructor said you were doing fine. I'll back that up. Good Luck! And don't lose your nerve."

Dean's urge to fly may have been the product of no more that boyish dreams, but now that he had been up in an airplane, he knew without a doubt that he wanted to fly. But the next two days were laden with anxiety of the consequences for his foolish acts—here he was facing not only demotion, but he was also liable to be court-martialed.

Then came the day of reckoning. He was ordered to report to the post commander. Feeling himself already condemned, he forced himself to enter the C.O.'s outer office where he was greeted with nothing but cold expressions as he passed from the sergeant major to the adjutant. The major led the way down the hall and into a large office. Behind the desk sat a craggy-faced man with the silver leaf of a lieutenant colonel on his shoulders.

The adjutant saluted and laid the file of papers on the desk, saying, "It's the Sergeant Smith case." Dean stepped up, saluted, and stood at stiff attention. The colonel returned his salute, then studied the papers a bit, then asked, "How do you like flying?"

"Very much sir."

"You want to become a pilot."

"Yes sir." As he remembered Joe-Ben's advice. He added, "I would rather have a pair of wings like yours, sir, than anything else in the world."

"Damn silly way to go about it, cooking up all this rigamarole." The colonel went on to ask many questions about Dean's background. Then suddenly he said, "I'm favorably disposed toward any young man who wants to learn to fly."

The colonel then turned to the adjutant. "Put in the School Report File that Sergeant Smith has been given a reprimand. But don't put it in his personnel record—not unless he gives us further trouble. Oh yes, and give him the application forms for flying cadet. You might have Sergeant Jones show him how to fill them out. He has now been orally examined and his qualifications found satisfactory."

The colonel then turned back to Dean. "You still have a long row to hoe. The physical examination is severe. Ground school is worse. If you bust out of ground school, I'll see that you dig ditches for the rest of the war. That is all."

Dean was ecstatic. Suddenly the world had changed for him. With his heart pumping like a speeding machine, his feet seemed to glide above the floor as he followed the adjutant out of the office and down the corridor to the reception area.

Sergeant Jones proceeded to show him how to fill out the application which required a minimum age of nineteen years and six months, and two years of college education. At this point Dean could do nothing but continue the charade. Without hesitation he jauntily inscribed that he had graduated from a junior college, which indeed he had, but only from its high school department; he set back his birth date still another year, which made him almost twenty. He now had three ages to keep track of, including his real one. Luckily, no one ever compared the records, so from that point on, nothing slowed him down from getting his commission as a shavetail pilot or from advancing to a dream position as a certified instructor in the United States Army Air Service.

Ace of the Escadrille

Of all the volunteers in the *Lafayette Escadrille*, the most outstanding member was Raoul Lufbery, a short, muscular, and quiet adventurer with no basic roots or family ties, and little formal education. Although French-born, he claimed Wallingford, Connecticut home, and gained citizenship by serving with the U.S. Army in the Philippines before World War I. After his enlistment was up, he traveled to the Orient, became acquainted with the noted French aviator Marc Pourpe, and signed on as a mechanic to barnstorm around Europe and Africa. When war broke out on the Continent the summer of 1914, Pourpe offered his services to the French air corps, and Lufbery, out of a job, was among the first Americans to volunteer for the French Foreign Legion; he had requested assignment as an aviation mechanic, and within a week was back with his friend again.

Three months later Pourpe was killed in action. Lufbery was shaken by his friend's death, and it didn't take more than a suggestion for him to switch to pilot training. At first he showed little skill in bomber training and slow learning for pursuit, but he persisted until gaining proficiency enough to join the all-American *Lafayette Escadrille* on May 24, 1916.

Two months passed before he scored his first victory, but with two kills the same day he was off to a remarkable air-war career. From that time on he became a relentless stalker, prowling the sky for hours, never returning until his fuel or ammunition were exhausted. At first he was not a skilled duelist for he often landed with his Nieuport full of bullet holes and shrapnel tears. However, his luck held out, and by the fall of that year his fifth kill made him the first ace of the group.

Although Luf tended to be a loner, he never failed to look out for his comrades, and saved some from certain death on several occasions.

His zeal for flying and the care he took with his plane made him one of the most respected pilots on the Western Front, and his victories, no doubt, did much to make the *Escadrille* a living legend. The group's record may not have influenced the United States to enter the war as the French had hoped, but there was no doubt that it inspired large numbers of young Americans to enlist in the American Air Service.

Shortly after the United States did enter the war, the top officials broke up the *Escadrille* and other squadrons in spite of great protest from the pilots. They all felt they were better off with an organization that was armed, experienced, and trained for fighting in the sky instead of being mixed with a bunch of eager newcomers. The war was not going well for the Allies, and just when the experienced pilots were needed most, the men of the old *Lafayette Escadrille* were doomed to wander about inactive airfields that had no planes, mingle with men who had no war experience, and sip the dregs of enforced idleness.

Lufbery was commissioned a major and assigned to the 94th Pursuit Squadron where he had little to do except instructing and paper shuffling. He knew he was not earning his pay and that he was of little use to the war effort. He resented the position he was in and yearned to be back in action.

Finally his spirits picked up when members of his squadron downed two German planes. Psychologically, it was a great boost to the Allied morale, and Lufbery nurtured the enthusiasm with daily training and talks with the pilots. Of all the questions posed to him, he recounted that his major fear was the dread of fire in the air. Unlike the German pilots, the allied flyers had no parachutes. The only alternative to jumping was to sideslip the machine in the hope of preventing the flames from burning the main spars and wings before the pilot could bring the plane to a safe landing.

On May 19, 1918 he was forced into this dreaded situation. A German photographic plane appeared over his field, and Lufbery acted instinctively. His own airplane was temporarily out of commission so he climbed into a combat-ready Nieuport and took off. The German plane passed closely enough to the ground that the pilot and observer could be plainly seen, and Lufbery was right behind them at unbelievable speed. Coming straight up on the tail, he fired four or five bursts, but the German did not reply. Lufbery then seemed to be having some trouble with his guns and climbed while trying to clear them, then dove straight for the enemy, firing again. This time the German replied with gunfire, and the Nieuport drew off gradually before turning upside down. From the ground it looked like a filled sack falling out, as smoke and flames began to streak from the plane.

What looked like a sack was Lufbery himself. Some believed he jumped to avoid the flames, but General 'Billy' Mitchell later related that eye witnesses reported the pilot falling before the flames began to appear, so he believed that Lufbery, in his hurry, had failed to tie himself in with his belt; the German shots cut his controls—his airplane turned over and he fell out. Without a parachute he didn't have a chance.

Lufbery landed at the rear of an old shoemaker's house near the Moselle river. The yard was typical rural French with farm animals, and flowers fringing along a white picket fence. It was this fence that broke his fall, but he was dead by the time the shoemaker's daughter got there. She immediately recognized him, for he was a great hero among the French peasants, as his mother had been one of them. The girl immediately covered the body with flowers from the yard, then waited for others to come and carry the fallen pilot to the town hall.

On May 20th, as fellow pilots surrounded the casket piled high with flowers, several generals gave short addresses and paid their last respects. As Raoul Lufbery was laid to rest in the little cemetery beyond the Sebastapol Hospital, airplanes of the 1st Pursuit Group, led by Eddie Rickenbacker, flew overhead and dropped flowers, paying a final tribute to one of the greatest heroes of the war.

The Maverick Devastator

Perhaps the most flamboyant of all American pilots at the front was Frank Luke, the 'wild man' from Arizona. At first Luke wanted no part of the war, but was persuaded to enlist by his sister, who was a nurse. He started with the U.S. Signal Corps, but soon applied for training in the Aviation Section. To his amazement he was accepted, then trained in Texas and California before being commissioned a second lieutenant on January 23rd, of 1918. Following a short leave, he sailed from New York for France on March 4th.

Upon arrival he received advanced training in flying and aerial gunnery, then logged considerable flying time in service-type aircraft. But this failed to satisfy the outspoken Luke; he wanted some action and demanded a position with a front-line squadron.

After repeatedly complaining, he was finally sent to the 27th Pursuit Squadron at Saintes, France. Right from the start he was in trouble. He resented any advice, military discipline, or regulations. On one flight he deserted his formation to go prowling about on his own. He claimed to have shot down a German Albatross, but no one believed him, and his claim was denied. Fellow pilots lost respect for him, and from then on he deserted his formation on any pretext possible. His commander, Major Hartney, knew he had a maverick to contend with, but figured he would let him have his way for a while to see what would come about.

There was another outcast of strong-willed German descent in the squadron, Joseph Fritz Wehner. It seemed that he and Luke had quite a bit in common and they teamed up to become one of the most devastating duos in the air.

For some unknown reason Luke was attracted to destroying enemy kite balloons. Some other pilots believed they were more difficult and unsafe to shoot down because they were heavily guarded. Whatever the reason, Luke, with the help of Wehner, was death on the balloons. The two went up on September 14th to attack a balloon near Buzy. Luke sent it down in flames while Wehner fought off a formation of eight Fokkers. Once the intruders had been driven away, Luke set off by himself to knock down another gas bag over Boinville.

The following day the two pilots went aloft again, but became separated. Luke downed a balloon near Boinville, then attacked a second over Bois d' Hingry. Upon turning away he was attacked by seven Fokkers. Fortunately, Wehner, who had downed a balloon himself near Verdun, spotted the action and flew like the devil to shoot two of the enemy off Luke's tail. That same afternoon Luke went up alone and downed another *Drachen*—totaling six balloons in three days. On the evening of September 16th, three more kites fell before the guns of the fighting duo.

On September 18th they spotted two balloons near Labeuville, and going down, with Wehner protecting his tail, Luke destroyed both observation gas bags. Zooming away from the kill, he saw his comrade engage with a flight of six Fokkers, and joined in, shooting down two of the enemy aircraft. In the melee he lost sight of his pal, and assumed he had escaped, so he turned to head deeper into German Territory to see a flight of Spads attacking a Halberstadt. Luke gunned his engine and went right through the French formation like a hawk after prey, and sent the enemy plane down in flames.

In a brief period of time he had made a remarkable number of kills, but his elation turned to gloom when he landed and learned that Wehner had been shot down and killed. Group Commander Hartney, conferring with General 'Billy' Mitchell, decided it was best to send Luke to Paris for a fourteen-day furlough, to relax and escape the depression from the loss of his friend.

But Luke was back in a matter of days, complaining that there was nothing to do in Paris. Bewildered by the remark, his commander allowed him to see action again, and on September 26th he went out after another *Drachen* with Lieutenant Ivan Roberts.

Luke got the balloon, but Roberts was shot down during the attack. This further depressed Luke and he immediately went AWOL.

Upon his return he was ordered to stay on the ground, but quickly disobeyed and took off once more in his Spad and landed at a foreward emergency field to refuel before heading across the German line. His commander ordered Luke's immediate arrest, but before anyone could catch him, he was in the air once again. Circling the American balloon headquarters at Souilly, he dropped a note that read:

"Watch those three Hun balloons along the Meuse."

Luke

It was an amazing exhibition that brought everyone out on the 27th's field, including General Mitchell, who watched with binoculars. Luke sent down the first balloon at Dunsur-Meuse, then a second at Briere Farm. During this second attack he was wounded, but flew on to Milly to bring the third down in flames. Then he went on to strafe German troops in the streets of Murvaux before being forced down in the outskirts of the village.

Though severely wounded, he managed to reach a meadow area, safely land, and climb from his cockpit in an attempt to reach a small cemetery. A platoon of German infantrymen intercepted and gave him a chance to surrender, but the defiant Luke refused, choosing to shoot it out with his .45 service pistol. It was a hopeless gesture, and he went down in a hail of rifle fire.

In just seventeen days, Frank Luke had set a remarkable record of downing at least three planes and fifteen balloons—his habit of making unauthorized sorties led to some confusion over the actual score. And though he was criticized for being headstrong and a maverick, his daring bravery against great odds was finally recognized, posthumously, by the nation's highest military award, the Congressional Medal of Honor.

Ace of Aces

Of all the pilots in the U.S. Air Service on the Western Front, none topped Captain 'Eddie' Rickenbacker—but he didn't start out that way.

He was a skilled driver on the motorcar track, and entered the war as General Pershing's personal chauffeur, but soon after reaching France, Colonel 'Billy' Mitchell happened to see Rick's mechanical ability firsthand, and suggested that he would be more valuable in the Air Service.

General Pershing didn't agree, and thought that, at nearly twenty-seven years of age, Rick was too old for such craziness. But Rick liked the idea, and persisted until the General gave him a transfer to receive flight training with the 2nd Aviation unit at Tours.

Rick's knowledge of engines overshadowed his skill in the cockpit, so he was made Chief Engineering Officer of the 3rd A.I.C. at Issodun. With this new position, he continued his flight and gunnery training and finally grew proficient enough to join the newly-formed 94th Aero Pursuit Squadron.

On March 6th Rickenbacker had his first taste of front line flying. Under the watchful eye of ace flier Major Raoul Lufbery, he and Doug Campbell ventured into German territory. This flight brought Rick many anxious moments—first he was flying a cast-off French Nieuport; worse, it was unarmed; then they were going through anti-aircraft fire; and suddenly he was airsick. He wasn't prepared for any of this.

As soon as he landed back at the airfield, he knew he had to do something about his weaknesses. First he absorbed all of the flying knowledge he could from Lufbery. And then he flew hour after hour, practicing corkscrew maneuvers until he felt nauseated. Over and over he repeated the procedure until one wonderful day there was no more airsickness. He had won his first battle.

After long days of inaction, a supply of guns, ammunition, instruments, flying clothes, spare parts, and new planes arrived. The group immediately moved up to the front, ready to be the first American squadron to go into action.

The honor deserved a distinctive insignia. All of the pilots offered ideas. Major Haffer, the CO, suggested Uncle Sam's stovepipe hat with stars and stripes for a hatband. Flight surgeon Lieutenant Walters mentioned the old American custom of throwing a hat into a ring as an invitation to battle. And thus was born one of the most famous military insignias of all time—the Hat-in-the-Ring emblem of the Flying 94th.

On April 14th, Captain Peterson, Lieutenant Reed Chambers, and Rickenbacker took off with the new insignia proudly emblazoned on their Nieuports—the first combat mission ever ordered by an American commander. It nearly turned into a fiasco. The fog was so heavy that Peterson turned back. Reed and Rickenbacker became separated and nearly lost. Then two German planes which were pursuing them evidently became lost. On the ground, Doug Campbell and Allen Winslow heard the the German planes overhead, and took off for an attack, shooting one of them down and forcing the other to land. News of the 94th double victory was flashed back to the States; the 94th was in the headlines. Luckily for the German pilots, neither of them were seriously injured.

During the next few days Rickenbacker had some close shaves and was lucky enough to live through them. As far as action was concerned, he was disappointed, but the lessons learned were to be invaluable in future skirmishes.

It was April 29th before he brought down his first enemy airplane, and as soon as he landed, the whole gang came out to congratulate him. There was never a closer fraternity than the group of the 94th.

The Squadron ran up five straight victories before the inevitable happened. Charley Chapman was killed when he went out with three other pilots and attacked five Pfalz fighters. During the fight, Chapman dove on a German two-seater, then a Pfalz got on his tail. Charley pulled out of his dive to meet his pursuer and flew right into a burst of gunfire from the two-seater. Within seconds the entire Nieuport was in flames. The toll continued—within days Hall was shot down and captured, and then Lufbery was shot down and killed.

With more hours in the air than any other American flier, Rickenbacker took over as commander. By now he had given a great deal of thought to new techniques and strategies which would help him survive. One night he and Chambers were hashing over new ideas and came up with one so simple that they wondered why no one had thought of it before. Their plan was simply to take off well before dawn, climb as high as their Nieuports would take them, and hover high over the lines—waiting for the first German plane to come by.

On a chilly morning, the last day of May, the two took off shortly after 4 A.M., climbed to 18,000 feet, and circled in the below zero temperature. Dawn came on a beautiful cloudless day. Their scheme had worked perfectly, except for one thing—the predictable Germans had not shown up to photograph the Allied lines.

Apparently Reed had given up and gone home, so Rick figured he would try a new hunting ground. Twenty-five miles to the east was the famous old fortress city of Metz, with a German aerodrome nearby. Rick climbed to 20,000 feet and flew over the area several times, but the enemy simply was not flying that day. With not much gas left, he cut his engine and silently circled the field like a great bird of prey. Far below, three graceful German Albatrosses taxied out onto the field and lifted off. One by one they headed southward, climbing steadily, obviously unaware of Rick's presence above them.

Rick hoped to catch them over the lines and began a shallow dive to start the propeller going, then turned on the ignition. He gunned the engine and started his approach to the rearmost Albatross. So intent was he on the pursuit, he had forgotten the enemy stratagem. Suddenly, black puffs appeared in the sky. The German batteries had seen him, and it was their way of warning that the enemy was overhead.

All three German pilots immediately put their planes into a dive. Rick had no intention of letting them get away, and in the excitement he forgot the Nieuport's fatal weakness of shedding its wing covering in a hard dive. He gunned the engine up to a speed of at least 150 miles an hour and closed in on the last plane. At fifty yards out he gave a 10-second burst of machine gun fire and saw the bullets hit the plane. The pilot had made a stupid mistake of diving rather than trying to outmaneuver the enemy.

As soon as Rick saw the German plane go out of control, he tried to pull out of the dive to put the ship into a sharp climb and have it out with the other two. He pulled the stick back into his lap only to hear a ripping, tearing crash that shook the plane. The entire spread of linen over the upper right wing was stripped off by the force of the wind. He manipulated the controls, but it did no good. The plane turned over on her right side, the tail went up, and the ship went into a tailspin. With the nose down, the tail began revolving faster and faster until it looked like sure death. As if he wasn't in enough trouble, the two remaining Albatrosses began their attack, pumping bullets into the helpless Nieuport. A crippled plane can take a long time to flutter to earth, and Rick wondered exactly how he would die—hit with bullets, torched by flames, or mashed into the ground?

The earth was coming up fast. As a last ditch effort he pulled open the throttle. The sudden speed lifted the nose of the plane, and for a second it was horizontal. He pulled the joy stick and reversed the rudder, which must have been one combination in a million that would work, for the plane remained almost horizontal. He was headed for the Allied lines only a couple of miles away. If only he could hold it like that, he might make it.

At less than two thousand feet, every antiaircraft battery, every machine gunner, and it seemed like every rifleman, began sending a curtain of lead in his direction. Having no other choice, he flew right through it all.

With the engine going full throttle and the controls jammed in the only position that enabled it to stay aloft, the little plane and pilot reached home base at treetop level. Everyone on the ground rushed out to see what fool was coming in at such speed. The plane grazed the top of the hangar, pancaked down on the ground, and slid to a stop in a cloud of dust.

Swinging down from the bullet-riddled, battered little crate, Rick tried to saunter nonchalantly toward the barracks as though he came in that way every day. He felt perfectly calm until he reached his bunk. Like his other close calls, he experienced fear only after it was all over. Suddenly his knees turned to water, and he could no longer stand up. The fact that he was still alive finally overwhelmed him.

There was no trouble in validating his aerial victory, for the Albatross, with the dead pilot slumped over the stick, miraculously continued over the American lines and landed itself. This was Rick's fifth victory, gaining him membership in the elite group of American Aces. He went on to claim one victory after another—racking up his twenty-sixth by the 30th of October.

The last victory of the Flying 94th came on November 10th, one day before the Armistice. The Hat-in-the-Ring Squadron had downed 69 enemy planes, more than any other American outfit.

The morning of the Armistice, Rick was flying over the lines, and he could see an occasional muzzle flash from the ground—some of the enemy were shooting at him. Then at 11:00 A.M., both sides of no-man's land erupted. Brown-uniformed men poured out of the American trenches, gray-green out of the German. Helmets were thrown into the air, and soldiers were running everywhere, gray mixing with brown. Only seconds before, they had been willing to shoot each other; now all was jubilation. The war was over, and the American Ace of Aces had the best seat in the house.

U.S.MAIL
U.S. MAIL

Chapter

5

Blazing New Frontiers

De Haviland Mail Plane

With the exception of a few token attempts at establishing air transportation, it wasn't until after the war that man's dreams of business trips, air cargo, and mail service began to be realized.

During an early-day air mail experiment at the 1911 Belmont Meet on Long Island, Earl Ovington and his Bleriot Monoplane transported the mail each day over a six-mile route, but by the end of the week he was out of business; the show was over and the crowd had gone on its way.

The first scheduled air passenger service was started in California in 1913 by Silas Christofferson piloting his hydroplane between the harbors of San Francisco and Oakland. But, within a year and a half he and his brother had moved on after amassing $85,000 from their service—it was enough money to set up a new operation in Redwood City for instruction and plane building to cater to foreign nations.

A more publicized passenger service was offered in Florida on the 1st day of January in 1914. The St. Petersburg-Tampa Airboat Line with its entire fleet of one wooden-hulled Benoist flying boat piloted by Tony Jannus, began operation with two eighteen-mile round trips daily, carrying two passengers each way for a charge of $10 per round trip ticket. During the first month of operation the plane made 97 trips across the bay, carrying 184 passengers. The response from tourists was so great that two more planes were added within the year, but the volume was not sufficient to continue operation, and it wasn't long before the venture flew into oblivion.

Despite these early attempts at commercial aviation, the general public, and even informed individuals, viewed its future with a jaundiced eye. As far as most American entrepreneurs were concerned, neither the means nor the demand to sustain passenger or freight business existed early on; and once war was declared, the military contracts allowed little time to think about anything else.

During the war years, great advancements in airplane design were made, but they were entirely of military nature. Nothing was done to develop transport planes of any sort, and by the time the Armistice was signed in 1918, the United States had not a single machine capable of carrying passengers in anything but a most primitive fashion.

The first breakthrough in commercial flight was not by private companies, but by the Army Air Service. In the spring of 1918, the federal government called for bids to establish the nation's first aerial mail service. When there was no response from the private sector, the War Department provided military aircraft and pilots to fly the first air mail route between Washington, D.C. and New York City. With untrained pilots and converted Curtiss *Jennys*, the Aerial Mail Service got off to a very shaky start, but was successful enough to gain continuing support of Congress and the country.

The very existence of the air mail depended upon speed and reliability. Schedules had to be kept, mail trains had to be beaten, and the elements had to be conquered. Uncle Sam needed pilots, and the only ones available were the flyers recently mustered out of the service and looking for work. For them it was a glorious opportunity to continue flying.

Decked out in leather coats with badges emblazoned "U.S. Aerial Mail Service", the mail pilots were imposing figures, but they had their work cut out for them. This was a new frontier, and adventures to come would be as thrilling as any that ever beset the Pony Express riders. No maps existed to guide the way and all they had was their ability to recognize every town, river, mountain, and farm along the way. Uncle Sam would not tolerate any fair weather flyers, so they had to master the fog and rain in spring, thunderstorms in summer, still denser fog and rainstorms in fall, then blizzards and cold in winter. Besides the weather problems there was always the possiblity of mechanical troubles. Modified DeHavilands replaced the *Jennys*; their Liberty engines were powered with 380 horses, but they were also prone to quit at the most inopportune moments. The only safe recourse was to head for an opening, protect the mail, and load it aboard a train for safe delivery. Forced landings and crack-ups were not infrequent experiences as there were two or three every week in spite of the long hours of grueling work performed by the mechanics and maintenance men. Pilots learned by trial and failure, and every time one fell in the line of duty, a hard lesson was learned to pass on to the newcomers.

By September of 1920, mail was being delivered from coast-to-coast—aviation had crossed the threshold into a new era. The prohibition days to follow gave a boost to commercial aviation when pilots braved stormy weather and long distances to run illicit spirits over the nation's borders. It only stood to reason: if liquor could be safely carried by air, why couldn't passengers and express. Suddenly there was great potential for legitimate commercial air service.

Congressional passage of the Air Commerce Act of 1926 placed commercial aviation under federal regulation. The Act provided for the establishment of civil airways with lights, emergency fields, beacons and other navigational aids; the inspection and licensing of aircraft, the establishment of rules and regulations governing their construction; the licensing of pilots; the charting of airways and the publication of maps; and the promotion of aerial transportation—all vitally needed for safety and to stimulate the industry.

But the greatest obstacle to large-scale air transportation in America was the lack of proper air vehicles. The increasing demand for more seats and cargo space created a need for larger and more efficient aircraft. Among the more notable planes designed to fill this requirement was the Boeing *40A*, a rugged biplane developed expressly for regular transcontinental air mail service. Powered by a 400-hp Pratt & Whitney Wasp engine, the *40* cruised at 100 miles per hour and carried two passengers in a small compartment behind the engine. While the pilot braved the elements in the open cockpit, the passengers were snug and dry, but suffered from the cramped quarters and deafening engine noise. The *40B* was developed to increase the passenger load to four, but there was little improvement in their comfort.

C
742K
BOEING

These moves by the government and industry made commercial aviation look more promising, but it took the romantic impact of one lone flyer to make the nation truly air-minded. On April 21, 1927 the Atlantic Ocean was bridged by Charles Lindbergh flying his Ryan monoplane, the *Spirit of St. Louis* solo from New York to Paris. This marvelous achievement captured world-wide attention and provided the single greatest boost aviation had ever known. Almost overnight the financial and technical climate changed to set the stage for large-scale development of aviation in America. Within a year, applications for private pilot's licenses jumped from 1,800 to 5,500, the nation's still-fledgling airlines doubled their route-miles flown, tripled the value of mail hauled, and quadrupled the number of passengers carried. Independent airlines sprung up all around the country. Few of the them made money just hauling passengers, but they hoped to hang on long enough to get a crack at the lucrative mail contracts from the Post Office Department. Out of the pack emerged such industry leaders as Transcontinental Air Transport, Western Air Express, Varney Airlines, National Air Transport, American Airways, United Air Lines, and Eastern Air Transport.

Services began to expand beyond transporting only passengers and mail to hauling cargo, agricultural dusting, aerial photography, and fire watch. Airplane and equipment improvements opened the wilderness and backcountry areas of Alaska and the Western states that heretofore were forbidding to the hardiest of pioneers in earlier times.

The demand for more capacity, improved passenger comfort, and safety brought forth one of the most durable planes ever built, the Ford Tri-Motor, more affectionately known as the *Tin Goose*. A comparative featherweight, the attributes of this all-metal plane were its flying ease and capability to lift heavy loads out of small fields. The trimotor was used by all major airlines throughout the United States during the late 1920s and early 30s, and in spite of the fact that production ceased in 1932, dozens of the original 199 constructed remained in service for years, transporting passengers, cargo, and smokejumpers.

Within three years after Lindbergh's transatlantic flight, aviation had improved immensely. More passengers were being carried across America than all the rest of the world put together. More than half of the 181 airfields surveyed had some type of runway surfacing. Beacon lights guided the way, and radio was coming into its own to enable the pilots to fly through the murk.

The industry was flying high until January of 1934 when President Roosevelt, believing collusion of the airlines, ordered the system shut down. Postmaster General James Farley announced that all air mail contracts would be canceled at midnight February 19, 1934—thereafter, the Army Air Service was to fly the mail. Now any experienced pilot could have predicted what was going to happen. It was midwinter. Blizzards lashed the West, and gales, sleet, fog, and cold gripped the Middle West and East. Army pilots were not prepared for bad weather flying, nor were many trained for night flying. The Air Corps takeover rapidly turned into a fiasco. After fifty-seven accidents and twelve deaths in seventy-five days, the airlines were back carrying the mail—contracts were reinstated, but the industry was required to reorganize to eliminate conflicts of interest.

Out of this grew a new demand for yet larger aircraft which gave birth in 1934 to the Donald Douglas DC-2, a new design that flew from coast-to-coast in a record-shattering 13 hours to outperform anything in the air at the time. More notable was the next year when Douglas brought out his DC-3, the *Queen of the Skies*, a plane destined to become the most popular transport ever created, and there is little question that it did more for the advancement of commercial aviation than any single aircraft ever built. Here was a plane able to carry 21 passengers at 180 miles per hour through and above the weather, in comfort and incomparable safety. With flying time slashed in half, boosting ticket sales to all time highs, DC-3s were used on virtually every scheduled airline in the world. Its ruggedness gave it an unparalleled life span; out of the original 11,000 built, thousands remained in service for years to lead the way into new eras of air transportation.

Reflecting back, it is pretty remarkable the strides that were made by industry in less than two decades.....

Off to a Very Shaky Start

In the spring of 1918, President Wilson's Cabinet had decided on the establishment of an aerial mail service. Bids were called for, but none were received, so it was decided to order the Army to fly the mail as a training exercise. Congress appropriated $100,000 for a joint operation between the Post Office and War Departments, and on May 3rd of 1918, an order was issued to the Air Service to inaugurate the nation's first air mail service between Washington D.C. and New York City, with an intermediate landing at Philadelphia. There were to be flights every day but Sunday over the 218-mile route—and service was to begin at 11:00 A.M. on Wednesday, just twelve days from the date of notice.

Major Reuben Fleet, appointed Officer-in-Charge of the Aerial Mail Service, reported that there were no airplanes capable of flying non-stop from Washington to Philadelphia or from Philadelphia to New York; there was no way that they could be ready on such short notice. But any delay was out of the question. Invitation cards announcing the initial flight from Belmont Park in New York City had been printed and sent out to the press. Now, the War Department was obliged to fulfill the bureaucratic order, even if the pilots had to land in open fields enroute to retank with gasoline, oil, and water.

Major Fleet promptly ordered six JN-6Hs from the Curtiss Aeroplane Company on Long Island. The planes were to be modified, with the front seats and controls removed, substituting a hopper to carry the mail—and delivery was to be in eight days.

Engineers, mechanics, and pilots worked day and night, yet on the afternoon of May 14th, only two planes were operable.

Fleet had personally selected Lieutenants Howard Culver, Torrey Webb, Walter Miller, and Steven Bonsal as dependable pilots for the inaugural flights, but high-level politics intervened and changed his plans. The Post Office Department requested that Lt. George Boyle pilot the first flight from Washington D.C., and Lt. James Edgerton fly the first trip from New York City.

With Fleet following in a trainer, Edgerton and Culver left Belmont Park Race Track in the two modified planes the afternoon of May 14th. The weather was frightful, due to heavy fog. That was only the beginning of their troubles—they were plagued with engine problems, a fuel leak, and running out of gas. Working through the night they were able to get one machine in operation, and reached Washingon, D.C. at 10:35 A.M.. There was no air strip along the Potomac River, so the polo field had to be prepared for take off and landing. Since a row of 30-foot-high trees bordered the raceway, Fleet had to take it upon himself to remove a tree for clearance, for the Park Commission said it would take three months to act on such a request. Another obstacle was the bandstand on the end of the field, but nothing could be done about that. Fleet also had designated a Captain Lipsner, who had been detailed by Air Service Production, to have a supply of aviation fuel at the field for their arrival. Much to Fleet's anguish, the captain had not delivered one drop, so they had to drain gasoline from a British airplane and two American ones in order to have enough for their mail ship.

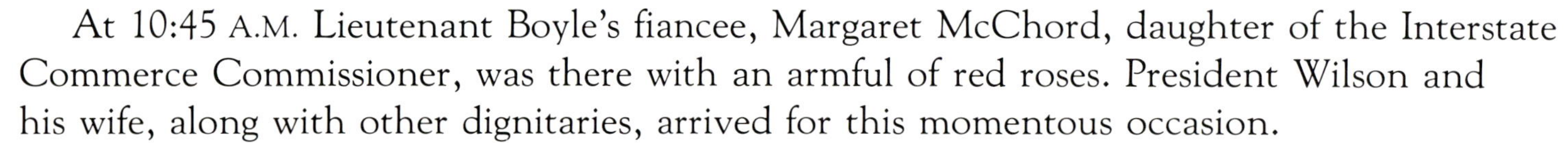

At 10:45 A.M. Lieutenant Boyle's fiancee, Margaret McChord, daughter of the Interstate Commerce Commissioner, was there with an armful of red roses. President Wilson and his wife, along with other dignitaries, arrived for this momentous occasion.

At the appointed hour, Major Fleet strapped his map to Boyle's leg and gave him the correct compass course to Philadelphia.

Margaret kissed her fiance goodbye and waved him off.

Boyle took off with no problem, but that was all that was good about the flight. He immediately got lost in the air, and landed in a plowed field near Waldorf, Maryland, 25 air miles from takeoff. While landing, the plane nosed over, breaking a propeller. He called back to Fleet for instructions, and was directed to bring the mail back to the field for air shipment the next day.

The Post Office Department then requested that Lieutenant Boyle be given another chance. This time Fleet accompanied him in another airplane for 40 miles on the correct compass course before turning him loose. Once again Boyle became lost, ran out of gas, and landed near the mouth of Chesapeake Bay where he refueled. Then he took off for Bustleton Field, but crashed near the Philadelphia Country Club. He wasn't hurt but the plane's wing was broken, and the mail had to be delivered by truck.

The Post Office Department then had the gall to request that Boyle be given a third chance. Without second thoughts, Fleet denied the request, stating that, "Lieut. Boyle is relieved of all duty with the Aerial Mail Service and is being sent back to flying school for further training in cross-country flying."

Although the flights from Washington to New York were disasterous, the inaugural was not a total loss, as Lieutenant Edgerton did manage to relay the southbound mail from Philadelphia to Washington on the afternoon of the 15th.

For the next four days, the mail service was busy, but then the novelty wore off, and the patronage steadily declined. Army pilots continued to fly the routes and carry the mail nearly three more months, but by then the War Department had had enough, and on August 12th, turned the operation back to the Post Office to carry on.

First Flight Out

Everyone considered flying the air mail the next thing to suicide, but a comfortable living could be made if one was around long enough to enjoy it.

The Aerial Mail Service was looking for experienced pilots, and Dean Smith, now out of work, figured he fit the bill. He had not changed his ways since he had conned his way into the Army, and had also finagled a commission as an officer in the Air Service before his eighteenth birthday, so when an air mail official asked him if he could fly a DeHaviland, he replied without hesitation, "I've never had any trouble with the plane."

And that was the truth, as he had never even flown one. After much query of the mechanics and some experimenting with a DH on the field, he got a pilot's job in the spring of 1920. Almost immediately, he was assigned to fly the route from Bellefonte, Pennsylvania to Cleveland, Ohio, and back again. Never having been to Cleveland, he asked the field manager for some flight maps, but all he got was a smile, because no such things existed. At least, he figured he could expect to make his first trip escorted by one of the Cleveland pilots, but he couldn't be so lucky. The best he could do was review Rand McNally road maps with senior pilot Max Miller and listen to him describe the land marks of towns, hills, rivers, roads, buildings, and race tracks all the way to Cleveland.

In a few days, he got his chance for his first run when the westbound came in and there was no other pilot available to take the mail on to Cleveland. It had been raining off and on all day, and low clouds were barely clearing the ridges; however, no one seemed concerned as they transferred the mail to his DH-4, so he warmed up the Liberty engine and took off to head for the gap in the first ridge to the west.

Max's instructions proved to be a big help. Dean made it over Rattlesnake Mountain and followed the river to Clearfield without much trouble. Veils of cloud cover forced him to twist and dodge along the route as the squalls grew heavier. By the time he reached the slope leading up to the plateau, the clouds were so solid that he had to turn back. The sky looked lighter to the north so he headed out over some of the wildest country in Pennsylvania where he was able to work his way west again by zigzagging from one opening to another. His altimeter showed close to 3,000 feet above sea level—plenty of room to clear the mountain, but he was barely skimming the tree tops. After half an hour the rain eased up and the cloud cover rose a little. Finally, he could relax a bit. He was feeling pretty good about himself and his first run when, suddenly, his engine stopped.

Generally there is some warning—a cough or a sputter or two, so the pilot has a chance to head for an open spot. However, when the timing gear in a Liberty engine fails, there is a sudden silence. Dean wasted no time in quickly twisting all the knobs and gadgets, but there was no response and the motor stayed dead. While his hands were trying to restart the engine, his eyes were searching for some sort of field to land in. All he could see was sharply rolling hills covered with trees. Then to his left, he noticed a small clearing in a cup-like basin. It was downwind, but his gliding radius didn't allow much choice, so he went for it.

To reach the clearing required a sharp, almost vertical S-turn, first left, then right, while killing just enough speed and altitude to land down-wind, and still miss a nearby cliff. One thing he didn't know was that the clearing was full of brush and weeds cloaking a three-foot-high ledge of rock directly in front of his landing spot.

The plane's undercarriage slammed into the ledge as he landed. The plane snapped like a whip, and Dean was catapulted into a long head-first dive, like being shot out of a cannon. Fortunately, he landed in the brush and rolled to a stop in a sitting position, the padded leather ring that rimmed the cockpit hanging from his neck. There he sat, with his seatbelt laying across his lap, still holding the rubber grip pulled loose from the control stick. Miraculously he had no broken bones, but the plane was piled in a heap, like a wad of crumpled wastepaper.

Except for the lone clearing, the place was a virtual wilderness. There was no sign of civilization anywhere, but after some exploration, he located a little-used path that led downhill to a dirt road which he followed until he came to a small cabin. There on a bench sat an elderly couple who offered a greeting. Dean proceeded to tell them about the accident, and they assured him that the rural mail carrier would be along shortly with his horse and rig and would willingly help him. To show their hospitality, the woman brought out a bowl of tiny wild strawberries, a jug of cream, and a loaf of fresh home-baked bread.

Surely enough, the mail carrier came along in due course, with a mare pulling an old-fashioned hack. The old man and the mail carrier helped Dean bring the mail down to the road and load it into the hack. There were only a few sacks—hardly a hundred pounds total. Luckily, not much to carry any distance. Leaving the crumpled plane behind, there was no question about it, the westbound air mail was not only going to be late, but very expensive that day.

After expressing his thanks and goodbyes to the old couple, Dean climbed in the hack and rode with the mail carrier to Pithole, a little town on the railroad. There the station master accepted the mail shipment, and Dean used his Post Office travel commission to get a ticket to Cleveland.

Once aboard the train he settled back to reflect on his first flight for the Postal Service; all in all it had turned into quite an experience for a beginner.

Transcontinental Air Mail Route

Air Mail Coast-to-Coast

In the winter of 1920-21, while pilots and ground crews were struggling with faulty equipment and fighting ice, snow, and foggy conditions to deliver the mail, the Post Office Department was having its own troubles. Accidents and pilot fatalities were at an all-time high, and in order to get support for expansion of the air mail, the Department needed to convince Congress and the public in general of the importance of moving the mail by air. Their only hope was to stage a colossal event, one that would demonstrate the importance of the Aerial Mail Service. Their plan was to attempt a continuous passage of mail across the entire continent. Until that time the air mail had been a discontinuous operation: each route of approximately 400 miles was a separate entity. Mail was speedily moved by air during the day, but then transferred to ground transportation for movement after dusk.

The strategy for the demonstration called for the mail to be flown from each coast, transferring from plane to plane until it reached the other terminal. This would entail night flying across the Central Plains, something that had never been done before, as there were no facilities, equipment, nor precedent for cross-country flying at night. Moreover, it was the worst time of year to attempt such a scheme. For these reasons, pilots were asked to volunteer for the night segments—Cheyenne, Wyoming to North Platte, Nebraska, North Platte to Omaha, and Omaha to Chicago.

On Washington's Birthday of 1921, two planes took off at dawn from New York heading west. Pilots Bill Hopson and Dean Smith were in Chicago awaiting the relay to pick up the westbound mail, due around dusk. The weather had been overcast all day; snow started falling just before the planes were scheduled to arrive. The air west of Chicago was full of flakes, and Iowa City reported steady snow flurries. Despite the dismal outlook, Bill Hopson, whose section arrived first, decided to give it a try.

He was back in a few minutes with a report that visibility was too poor to fly in broad daylight, let alone at night—both westbound flights would have to canceled.

Meanwhile, the first eastbound flight out of San Francisco turned into disaster when pilot W.E. Lewis stalled after take-off from Elko, Nevada, spun in, and was killed instantly.

Farr Nutter, piloting the second section, was still on track. Clearing the Sierra Nevadas at 12,000 feet, he let down at Reno to transfer the mail to Jack Eaton who flew it on to Salt Lake City. Jimmy Murray carried it from there on to Cheyenne; then Frank Yeager flew the first leg of darkness into North Platte, arriving at 7:50 that evening. By then, fifteen hours had been consumed since takeoff, and now there was a delay in schedule while mechanics repaired a broken tail skid. It was 10:44 before Jack Knight could take over and head east. Few lights were visible on the snow-covered plains that time of night, although at Lexington, Kearney, and Central City citizens kept bon fires burning to help guide his course. The cold and darkness were bad enough, but his greatest hazards were mental fatigue and the apprehension that goes with attempting the unknown.

Full light of the moon helped him stay on route the rest of the way to Omaha where he landed at 1:15 A.M.. He was glad to be through with flying that cold night.

After a welcomed hot cup of coffee, he asked, "Who's going on from here?"

The field manager had to tell him that the westbound flights out of Chicago had been canceled and no other pilots were available. This was a disheartening thought. After all the miles that had been covered, he wasn't about to give up the project and decided to give it a try even though he had never made the Chicago run before.

Taking off at 2:00 A.M., over unfamiliar territory, Jack planned to land at Des Moines, Iowa but snow on the field was so heavily drifted that he had to pass it by.

Upon reaching Iowa City and finding no lights or flares to mark the field, he circled and gunned his engine to wake the sleeping inhabitants of the town. Finally a glow of light burst from a field south of town. The watchman, who had no inkling at all of the special flight, heard the roar of the motor and lit a fuse, wondering what blamed fool was out flying on night like this.

Jack set the plane down for refueling, then waited for the first light of dawn to take to the air again. His arrival at Chicago at 8:40 A.M. was met with disbelief—all hope had been given up for anyone to make it through the storm. Now there was still a chance to salvage the undertaking.

A plane was made ready and Jack Webster flew the mail on to Cleveland. Then Ernie Allison took it the rest of the way to New York, landing at 4:40 in the afternoon—33 hours and 21 minutes after the first plane left San Francisco the previous morning. It was a glorious moment for the Aerial Mail Service. Because of Jack Knight's remarkable persistence, the transcontinental flight had been completed as planned. Publicity of this historic event brought the air mail and its pilots into the limelight. The daily flights and adventures were given more attention in the press than ever before. The Post Office Department achieved its purpose, and Congress immediately responded with enough money to light the way between Chicago and Cheyenne. The service was so well received, that by 1924 lighted airways guided the pilots all the way, from coast to coast.

Night Flight to the Windy City

The October night was coming on fast as the young pilot pushed the old DeHaviland north toward Peoria. Just a week before, he had lost a DH on this same route because he didn't have an extra flare, wing lights, or a beacon to go by. Tonight he was more than an hour late because of engine trouble in St. Louis.

The night flight shouldn't have been any trouble if the air fields had been lit with revolving beacons, boundary markers, and floodlights, but the Robertson Aircraft Corporation couldn't afford such luxuries. The company was paid by the pounds of mail they carried, and often the sacks weighed more than the letters inside. Their mail hauling between St. Louis and Chicago earned them barely enough to keep going from month to month, and their financial condition was so bad that their planes and engines were purchased from Army salvage.

This night their chief pilot, Charles Lindbergh, encountered fog rolling in a few miles northeast of Marseilles and the Illinois River. There was a thick fog bank ahead of him, and being unable to fly under it, he turned back and attempted to drop a flare and land; but after pulling the release handle nothing happened. Since the top of the fog was less than a thousand feet high, he decided to climb over it and continue along the route, hoping to find a hole to drop through. Then, if he could get under the clouds, he could pick up the Chicago beacon which the government had installed on the flyway.

Glowing patches showed where cities lay along the route. With these bright spots for guidance, he had little trouble in locating the outskirts of Chicago and the general area of the Maywood field, but 800 feet of fog concealed the powerful searchlights directed upward and the two barrels of gasoline burning to attract his attention. As much as he tried, he was unable to pinpoint the airfield's location.

After circling for half an hour, Lindy knew it was a lost cause to find an opening, so he headed west, hoping to pick up the east-west transcontinental beacons. All of that route was fogged in, too. By then he had discovered that the failure of his flare to drop was caused by slack in the release cable. The flare might still function if he pulled the cable instead of the release lever. Turning south toward the edge of the fog bank, he intended to follow his original plan of landing in some farmer's field by flare light. No sooner had he changed direction than his engine sputtered a few times and then cut out completely. His first thought was that the carburetor jets had clogged, because he should have had plenty of fuel remaining in his main tank. Little did he know that several days before, a mechanic had discovered a gas leak and replaced the 110-gallon tank with an 85-gallon one!

After failing to start the engine after another try, he switched over to the reserve tank. Instantly the engine fired, convincing him that the main tank was empty. Now he had twenty minutes of flying time left, not enough to reach clear area south of the Illinois River. Given the situation at hand, he decided on emergency measures. He shoved the flashlight into his pocket and started to climb, planning to parachute out as soon as the reserve tank went dry. He tried without success to open the mail pit so he could toss out the bags. When that failed, he changed tactics, assuming that if he let the tank run dry there would be little risk from fire. He continued to climb when suddenly a light appeared from the ground. It held but a brief few seconds, but that meant a break in the fog. Circling down to 1,200 feet, he pulled on the flare-release cable. This time it functioned, but only to illuminate the top of the solid fog cover into which it soon disappeared without showing a trace of the ground.

Seven minutes of fuel remained. Seeing the glow of a town through the fog, he turned toward open country and nosed the plane upward.

He was at 5,000 feet when the engine sputtered and died. Without hesitation, he stepped up on the cowling and went over the right side of the cockpit, pulling the rip-cord as soon as he was well away from the plane. After falling head downward, the risers jerked him into an upright position as the canopy snapped open.

Pulling the flashlight from his belt, he played it down toward the fog bank. The sudden sound of the airplane's engine startled him. Figuring the plane was out of fuel, he neglected to cut the switches. Apparently when the ship nosed down, a small supply of gas drained into the carburetor; now it was off on a pilotless solo flight. As soon as the plane came into sight, Lindy could see that it was headed for him. It was making a left spiral of about a mile in diameter, passing about three hundred yards in front of his chute.

Slipping the flashlight into the pocket of his flying suit, he grabbed the risers to steer his chute away from the plane's path as fast as he could.

The ship passed completely out of sight, but reappeared again in a few seconds, its rate of descent being about the same as Lindy's. Before reaching the fog bank, he counted five spirals, each a little farther away than the last.

Knowing that the ground was less than a thousand feet below, he reached for the flashlight but found it missing. In his excitement he hadn't pushed it far enough into his pocket. By now, he could see neither earth nor stars and had no idea what was under him. Holding his feet together, he guarded his face with his hands and waited.

No sooner could he see the outline of the ground than he was down—right in the middle of a cornfield, with the chute's canopy settling over the stalks. Rolling the chute up, he hurried down the corn row. In a few minutes he came upon a stubble field and some wagon tracks, which he followed to a farmyard a quarter mile away. First, a large barn loomed up in the haze, then in the distance a lighted window showed that someone was still up. He was headed toward a house when he noticed headlights from the road and a spotlight playing back and forth. Thinking that someone might have spotted the wreck of the plane, he walked over to the car.

Someone called out, "Did you hear that airplane?"

"I'm the pilot," Lindy said.

"An airplane just dove into the ground," the man went on, paying no attention to his answer. "Must be right near here. God it made a racket!" He kept searching with his spotlight, but the beam didn't show much in the haze.

"I'm the pilot," Lindy said again. "I was flying it." But he had to display his parachute before the words finally sank in and the spotlight quit moving.

He went on to explain what had happened. Then he got into the auto, and the group, with the farmer, began a quarter-hour search without success. Finally Lindy asked to use the farmer's telephone. The party line was jammed with voices, all talking about the airplane and giving opinions on where it had crashed. Finally he was able to break in and ask the operator to put in emergency calls to St. Louis and Chicago. No sooner had he hung up than the phone rang—three longs and a short.

"That's our ring!" exclaimed the farmer.

The plane had been located about two miles away. Everyone headed to the crash site. The DH was wound up in a ball-shaped mass. It had narrowly missed a farmhouse, hooked its left wings on a grain shock a quarter mile beyond, skidded along the ground for eighty yards, ripped through a fence, and come to rest at the edge of a cornfield. The mail compartment was split open and one sack had been thrown out, but the mail was intact.

By then the sheriff arrived and Lindy wasted no time in gathering up the sacks; he had a schedule to keep. Loading the pouches into the sheriff's car, they headed for town, arriving in time to get the mail aboard the 3:30 for Chicago. Only then could Lindy relax; he had done his best to keep on schedule.

Beyond the Call of Duty

On the night of August 22, 1930 Roy Warner was flying at 7,500 feet, carrying the mail for Varney Air Line on the Boise, Idaho to Pasco, Washington run. About halfway to his destination, he suddenly felt a spray hitting him in his face. It was the worst of possibilities, a leak in the fuel line.

Nothing could be more horrifying to a pilot than the prospect of a fire in flight. As luck would have it, he was flying over Northeast Oregon in the vicinity of an emergency field near Baker City. Realizing that if he throttled the motor a backfire might result, Roy attempted a steep power dive. There may not have been any fire, but the strong gasoline fumes which filled the cockpit were nearly as bad. He couldn't help but choke and become nauseated.

The situation was critical, but Roy Warner wasn't the type to abandon ship. He had the mail to deliver, and at the moment, that was more important than anything else in the world. He just sat there, side-slipping to dodge the fumes, making the best out of a bad situation, all the way to the peaceful quietness of the emergency landing strip.

Flashing his landing lights on, he cut his motor to land. Suddenly fire broke out and flames shot back, setting his trousers afire and burning his hand clutching the stick.

By then he was committed and much too low to jump; he had no other choice than to stay with the plane. On his landing approach, the fire spread, burning the fabric from the right wing. The ship started into a spin then hit on one wing, bounced into the air, and came to a stop right side up with the cockpit afire.

Roy jumped out gasping for fresh air, but no sooner had he gulped a few lungs full than he thought of the mail. Rushing back to the burning plane, he threw all of the bags to safety, then escaped just before the gas tank exploded and the plane was engulfed in a ball of fire.

Roy's clothes were partially burned off; worse yet, his hands were blistered and bleeding, his face was burned, and eyebrows and eyelashes were gone, but he was still on his feet and would not give up. Within hours he was in Pasco and getting ready for his run back to Boise. Other pilots persuaded the manager to let one of the other pilots fly the schedule and allow Roy to ride along.

Because of his exhibition of bravery and meritorious service in the line of duty, the Postal Service awarded him their highest honor—the Air Mail Medal of Honor, for the mail pilot's duty was to safeguard the mail and equipment, but no regulation ever suggested that he should deliberately risk blindness, disability, or death by climbing back into a blazing airplane whose gas tanks were about to explode, just to save the mail.

Saving Lives by the Book

For 'Jepp' Jeppesen, the desire to fly dated back as far as he could remember—around the age of three or four, when he stood outside watching the birds fly overhead, marveling at their aerial gyrations. By the time he was fourteen he had saved enough money from delivering newspapers and groceries to take an eight-minute plane ride in a Curtiss *Jenny*. On the way down, the pilot cut the motor, letting Jepp thrill to the view of the sun glinting through the maze of spars and ribs. With the support wires screaming, and his hair blowing in the wind, he was hooked. After that, the desire to fly was so great he couldn't wait to finish high school. Instead, he started hanging around Pearson Airfield in Vancouver, Washington, washing planes and sleeping in the hangar. After accumulating $500, he traded flight time for working around the airfield, and then soloed in November of 1927, after just 2 hours and 15 minutes in the air.

From then on, he was always around airplanes. He started barnstorming with some of the older pilots and mixed in a little wingwalking. During off times he took his *Jenny* a mile up over the Columbia River and then made long slow turns all the way down, just for the fun of it. The hum of the engine, the beat of the prop, and the wind playing sound with the wires were music to his ears, and sensations he would never forget.

It wasn't long before the *Jenny* just wasn't plane enough for what Jepp wanted to do, so he upgraded to an Eaglerock and started work as an instructor and performer with Tex Rankin and his flying circus. Then he got the itch to see some new country and barnstormed his way south to Dallas, Texas, and by accident landed a job with Fairchild

Aerial Surveys, photographing the Delta area and New Orleans. Another survey project pulled him farther south, to Old Mexico.

In 1930 he was back in Portland, Oregon flying the night mail for Varney Air Lines. He liked the night work—it paid twice as much as by day—and it led to a job as reserve co-pilot for Boeing Air Transport, flying experimental trimotors on their Salt Lake-Cheyenne and Salt Lake-Reno runs. The experience was good, but the limited number of hours was not at all satisfying to a pilot who craved flying, so he quit and returned to Fairchild—just as the Great Depression hit. The survey workload was dismal, so he didn't have to think twice about leaving. Even though times were tough, the mail still had to get through, so Jepp wasted no time in driving to Cheyenne to get back with flying on the transcontinental mail route.

Some of the worst weather conditions on record greeted him that winter of 1930. It was so nasty that pilots often found themselves flying from one emergency field to another, then sitting on the ground with only the mail sacks and their planes for company, waiting out the storm before pressing on again.

Like other pilots, Jepp had only Rand McNally road maps and experience to guide him along the route, as no radios or other modern directional systems yet existed. Worse than that, during periods of low visibility he was forced to 'hug the UP' —flying low over the Union Pacific tracks to guide his way. It was so cold that even the heat from the engine, the heavy flying suit, and his boots failed to keep him warm, and after four or five hours of flying in sub-zero temperatures, the mechanics had to about lift his near-frozen body from the open cockpit.

Eighteen pilots flew the route between Oakland and Cheyenne, and four of them were killed that winter; it was a high price to pay for keeping the mail on schedule.

This tragic record caused Jepp enough concern to take some immediate action so that he would not become just another statistic. Since nothing had ever been done on charting the airways, he took it upon himself to start jotting down information and sketching out letdown procedures for his own use.

The word got around on what he was doing, so whenever younger pilots asked the old-timers for advice, they would reply, "Go see Jepp. He's got it all written down."

After a number of inquiries, he began to foresee a major need for his information; that was the impetus he needed to gather more data for charting letdown procedures along all of the air mail routes. Driving from Chicago to Oakland, he checked out the emergency fields and obstructions around them, making note of different ways to get into them and how far they were away from the railroad tracks and highways. When he wasn't flying, he was traveling the countryside, climbing mountains and smokestacks, taking altimeter and temperature readings, all the while recording the information in his notebook. Data was gathered from every source imaginable, including city and county engineers, surveyors, farmers and ranchers. At first he planned to provide the collected information to the federal government and get them to do the final charting, but they showed no interest. After the frustration of getting nowhere with the bureaucracy, he found if anything was going to get done he would have to do it himself. Gathering up all of his notes and diagrams, he set out to print 50 letdown procedures and put them in a small notebook. For ten dollars the recipient was the proud owner of all the route information that Jepp had so carefully accumulated.

He really didn't start the business to make any money, just to preserve himself for old age. There was no single incident that fired him up to do all this documentation, but he had had enough scary experiences, and seen so many of his fellow pilots killed and injured, that he developed a great instinct for self-preservation and wanted to pass it on.

Elrey Jeppesen never gave up his obsession for aviation safety, and over the years continued collecting data and expanding letdown procedures. His original little black book evolved into an industry, and a ***Jeppesen Airway Manual*** has since become the best friend and companion a pilot could ever have.

Perils of the Bush

In 1932 Art Woodley was offering passenger and freight service to the Alaskan backcountry with the motto *Have Plane Will Travel*. The Woodley Airways was only a one-plane, one-pilot operation, but the service was outstanding. His specialty was a flight between Anchorage and Nome as an alternative to the dogsled journey which took a month and cost $750. Woodley charged $150 and the trip only took a day.

On September 24th of 1932, Harry Morton was helping Art load up his Diesel Bellanca for a trip over the Talkeetna mountain wilderness for Fairbanks.

After a good start they were well on their way when the old Diesel started acting up. Art knew that this was no place to have engine trouble so he headed the plane back to Anchorage but didn't get far before the motor quit completely. Luckily, there was a good spot where they could put down in the Chulitna River.

Since the ship was equipped with pontoons, everything was fine as they drifted along with the swift moving current, finally coming to rest around 4:30 in the afternoon. They found themselves high and dry on a sandbar, in the middle of the river. A light snow mixed with rain was falling, so they decided to settle down in the ship for the night.

The next day they tried repairing the motor but were having no luck, as it seemed that three of the pistons had melted. The only thing left to do was to try making it to shore and start walking the 20-some miles to Talkeetna, so they proceeded to shed their clothes and make for shore through the icy water.

After the first day's travel through the tall grass in continuous rain and wet snow, their clothing was soaked. When they stopped to build a fire and dry out, they found that their matches had gotten wet and were completely useless.

That night the temperature dropped below freezing, so they had to keep moving to survive. The route was brutal going since they couldn't follow the river's edge. They had to detour over the hills, through alder brush and devil's club, and over windfalls. For the next three days and nights they struggled on in sheer misery.

The weather cleared late in the afternoon of the 28th, and a search party, consisting of Alonzo Cope, Morton's son, Jack, and Charlie Rutan, left Anchorage in a Fairchild 71. If the weather held, Cope figured on flying for a couple of hours after dark to see if they could spot a fire. The party was out a little less than an hour when Charlie caught a glimpse of the Bellanca, still sitting on the sandbar. It was starting to snow, the fog was rolling in, and the darkness was rapidly coming on. Cope circled the ship, then headed downstream, still circling, looking for a firelight. The weather was thickening fast, and Al had all he could do to handle the plane while Jack and Charlie did the looking.

From their encampment on a small gravel bar in the river canyon, Art and Harry had heard the searchers as they passed overhead on their flight upstream, but they were unable to signal them. Having traveled for days through the storm, with no fire or food, except for some berries, they were exhausted. They had made their way about six miles downstream before stopping, and were now huddled together in a wet sleeping bag, trying to get some warmth from each other's bodies. They had a small flashlight, but it was buried in the bottom of the bag and they hadn't had enough time to get it out and signal for help.

The searchers were about to give up the hunt and head back to Anchorage, figuring on starting out again early the next morning. Just then, Charlie Rutan saw a flicker deep in the crooked river canyon.

Twice, Al Cope powered the plane between the 100 foot high walls. The canyon was only two hundred feet wide, and it was nearly pitch black with a bit of snow falling. He could see the little light moving frantically in the darkness, but he didn't know if it meant to land or go away. Finally, he decided to chance a landing, and it was a thriller! The river was crooked and the walls too high to slip over, so he had to approach from upstream and snake his way down the canyon course.

Just as he rounded a corner, looking for the light, he suddenly realized that he was nearly on the bank. Gunning the motor, and using lots of rudder and stick, he managed to get over to land right beside the two men, only to be taken downstream a quarter of a mile in the swift current. After bouncing over some boulders, he landed on an island of rocks. With the help of his companions, Cope got the ship turned around and then taxied back upstream against a strong tail wind. Just as they reached the two men, both pontoons bounced onto a rocky reef that was covered by fast moving water.

By now the temperature had dropped and hail began to fall. It sounded like it was tearing the fabric from the frame. Jack and Charlie, already wet to their waists from getting the plane turned around, jumped into the water again with rope in hand to secure the bow of the pontoons to a submerged log that was embedded in the sand and gravel.

The rescuers found Art Woodley out in the storm, stark naked, and Harry Morton huddled in the wet sleeping bag, too ill and exhausted to move. The party lost no time in getting the two men into the ship, making them as comfortable as possible with dry blankets. They were offered some hot soup and coffee, but the men were too exhausted and sick to eat. A spare sleeping bag was used as a bed for Harry. The others settled back in the cramped quarters to wait out the storm.

Before long, the rain and sleet let up and it turned bitter cold, with the temperature dropping to 12 above zero. It was a miserable night for everyone, sitting in cramped quarters, listening to the pontoons grinding on the rocky reef. Al Cope was afraid that the swift water would undermine the rocks they were sitting on, and leave the ship at the mercy of the current. He sat in the pilot's seat throughout the night to be ready to start the motor if the plane did go adrift. Periodically he checked outside to see if the ship was still secure. His hip boots kept him dry, but his feet nearly froze from the icy water.

Daylight finally came at about 7:00 A.M., and just as they expected, there was ice and frost covering the ship, and it would be mid-morning before the sun reached into the canyon to melt the coating. But they didn't waste any time in examining the pontoons for damage and found each had been punctured during the landing or taxiing the previous evening. They were filled up to the waterline and rested heavily on the rocks. This was disgusting! All night long they agonized about being set adrift; instead, they were solid on the bar. The way it was, they could have slept without a worry.

By using some rags and wooden plugs they were able to partially stop the leaks. Then they made everything ready while Al warmed up the motor. They pumped the pontoons as dry as they could, Charlie and Jack released the ropes, then shoved the ship out into the swift current. They both hung onto the pontoons and climbed into the cabin as Al gave the motor full throttle.

About 2,000 feet downstream was a reef across the river, and also a sharp turn of the canyon to the left. Al figured if he got the ship on the step of the floats as quickly as possible, it would go over the reef with no damage, and with high speed, he could make the sharp turn in the river.

The Fairchild was heavy with five people plus the emergency equipment. The pontoons were carrying a lot of water, and there was a little tail wind. As the ship roared down the river it gathered speed rapidly. Al was able to miss some large boulders easily, and with a lot of coaxing the ship got up on the step in time to clear the reef. The short turn to the left was followed by another to the right while they were still on the water.

By that time the ship was getting light and almost ready to fly. Al kept it down all the way through the canyon while he twisted and turned, gathering speed for the lift off. By the mouth of the canyon they were airborne—only then could they relax, for at last they were heading home and back to the comfort of civilization.

Old 249

The morning of December 15, 1922 found Hank Boonstra coaxing his DeHaviland mail plane No. 249 high in Utah's Uinta Mountains. He knew he had to reach 11,000 feet to clear Porcupine Ridge, but his carburetor was icing up and the big Liberty engine was giving him barely 9,400 feet of altitude. He suddenly realized that his only hope was to pray for an updraft to lift him over the ridge, as the canyon was too narrow to turn around for an escape and another try.

His prayers weren't answered that day, so all he could do was lift the plane's nose in a power stall and mush into the deep snow on the west slope. The landing gear collapsed on impact, and the lower wings and fuselage burrowed into the deep snow. Hank hurried to unfasten his safety belt, get out of his parachute harness, and worm his way up and out of the cockpit. The sub-zero cold bit into his face and began to numb his body as he worked to get the ship's compass out of the instrument panel with a screwdriver.

With compass free and tucked in his leather jacket pocket, he placed the pouch of registered mail under his arm, and started working his way down the slope.

It is terrifying to imagine the danger which faced the pilot. Here he was, over twenty miles airline from the nearest civilization, shoulder-deep in snow, and ill-prepared for any kind of ground travel in the dead of winter. The nearest town was Coalville, far to the west on the Weber River, halfway between the Wasatch and Unita Mountains. He knew there was no chance of rescue, for no one would even worry about him until he was overdue in Cheyenne. If he tried waiting around he surely would freeze to death. His only hope to stay alive was to seek some shelter.

Floundering in the deep snow, he took a compass heading toward Coalville and began what was to be an incredible journey. Hour after hour he wallowed through the snow. Often too tired to go on, he knew he must keep going to survive.

When he didn't show up in Cheyenne it didn't take long for search parties to take to the air. While Hank struggled in the deep snow, a dozen planes searched vainly through the maze of snow-locked canyons and icy ridges. The only company he had was a squawking magpie, which he later credited with saving his life, for it kept him awake until he reached the Ross Rigby ranch after thirty-six hours of struggling over the snowy terrain. A phone call from the ranch brought an end to what had been the longest concentrated air search in history. Hank Boonstra was given a hero's welcome, but for Old 249, it looked like it was doomed to end its days high on Porcupine Ridge. There was some talk about salvaging her, and even a party of Air Mail mechanics and local ranchers organized to look into the possibility, but that just didn't seem practical.

For 43 years the old DeHaviland lay on that bleak mountain slope, her parts exposed to the elements. The wing fabric and thin plywood of the fuselage didn't last long in such a harsh environment and were finally blown away by severe mountain winds.

Bill Hackbarth and some of his Air Mail Pioneer friends couldn't get Old 249 out of their minds, and in 1964 they initiated a plan which would attract the attention of the entire nation. They planned to retrieve the parts and reconstruct the plane, and then fly her to Washington D.C., just in time to commemorate the Golden Anniversary of the U.S. Air Mail.

Wesley Agaard, who owned the property where the wreckage rested, hauled out the 600 pounds of bits and pieces which were then trucked to Bill Hackbarth's shop in Santa Paula, California. Months of work were expended, and restoration was well under way when a brush fire consumed nearly everything in the shop but the engine. Most men probably would have given up, but the pioneer pilots were more determined than ever.

After expending some $80,000 in labor, $1,000 for a radiator, and $10,000 for the engine, the job was completed, and Bill Hackbarth took off in the summer of 1968 to retrace the old Air Mail route and fly over the crash site in the Uinta Mountains. After 23 stops, his coast-to-coast air journey ended with an escort of Army helicopters. He was given the signal to land, but the only airport which caught his eye turned out to be the Anacosta Naval Station on the wrong side of the Potomac River. Bill landed expertly between two barriers 300 feet apart, then seeing his mistake, promptly took off between the same barriers and flew across the river to Washington National Airport to be greeted by a crowd assembled especially for the occasion. When he taxied up and climbed from the cockpit, his white hair blowing in the wind, there was a long-lasting roar of applause for his commemorative journey. Postmaster General Marvin Watson took the mail sack offered him and said, "Your daring flight is in the very best tradition of the Air Mail."

Today, Old 249 hangs in the Smithsonian Air Museum along with the first plane flown by the Wright Brothers, Charles Lindbergh's *Spirit of St. Louis*, and other members of the elite. The pilots have left us, many stories have been lost or forgotten, but the ships live on as a lasting reminder of the danger, excitement, and glory of eras gone by.

Chapter

6

The Glory Years

After the Armistice, the country was awash with cheap airplanes along with thousands of out-of-work military pilots wondering what they were going to do for a living. The outcome was inevitable. Knowing no other profession, hundreds of these begoggled, dashing young airmen joined the ranks of the gypsy fliers to invade the American countryside. They introduced the wonder of flight to every man, woman, and child who ventured to their impromptu airfields—to one and all they pitched the thrill of the air. For only a dollar a minute, each and everyone could take a spin in one of their marvelous flying machines.

For the most part, none of these surplus machines were suitable for the stunting and passenger carrying required of them; but there was no other choice as nothing else existed. That didn't faze the gypsy fliers as they took to the air in mass. At first everything was rosy—people would pay for one or two rides, but when the novelty wore off, starvation threatened and the gypsies found it hard to survive. Many banded together to perform hair-raising displays of reckless aerobatics; then some recruited young women daredevils for wingwalking and parachuting to spice up the act —anything to bring back the crowds. But the cutthroat competition, failing economy, and increasing costs made it more difficult each year. Accidents, injuries, and aging aircraft added to their problems; then the death blow came from Congress when it passed the Air Commerce Act of 1926 to register and certify aircraft and regulate air traffic. What lack of funds and casualties among their own ranks could not accomplish, the Feds were in the process of doing. The carefree life of the gypsy flier was about over and it was the beginning of the end of the greatest flying era ever known.

Many of the barnstorming pilots lucky enough to have survived, settled down as the fixed-base operators or carried the mail. Those who couldn't shake the gypsy from their blood flew off to Hollywood or joined one of the aerial circuses to continue their free-wheeling antics. With performers changing from plane to plane, and then from plane to train, boat, car, and horseback, upside down flying and intentional crashes, the stunting became more outlandish each day. Besides thrilling the crowds, they made good money hopping rides. A whole new generation was introduced to flying by such groups as the Gates Flying Circus which lasted nearly a decade and carried from 90,000 to 175,000 passengers a year. They gave high rides and low rides, long rides and short rides, straight rides and stunt rides—any kind of ride desired. The long ride was $5.00 and the short ride $2.50—and it was short, for they hauled four passengers in a Hisso Standard, in, up, down, and out in less than a minute.

There is little question the barnstormers introduced and popularized flying to the masses along with accelerating the technical development of aircraft in the 1920s; but as the gypsy flyers drifted off into oblivion, the record seekers took over to spur aviation on into the next decade. With improved designs, better equipment, and new daring, pilot competition was keen to see who could fly faster, higher, and longer. Records were broken nearly as fast as they could be recorded.

Cal Rodgers set the stage for distance flying in 1911 with his 49-day flight across the nation. By 1921 the time had been reduced to less than 24 hours, and the new challenge was for longer distances and non-stop journeys. Business tycoons, caught up in the excitement, offered great prizes for new records of daring. One of the largest was the $25,000 offer by Raymond Orteig in 1919 for the first non-stop flight across the Atlantic Ocean. The prize went unclaimed for eight years because no engine was reliable enough to make the trip, but development of the 220-hp Wright Whirlwind engine made it possible for Charles Lindbergh and his *Spirit of St. Louis* to claim the prize in 1927. The first to circumnavigate the globe were the U.S. Army World Cruisers who thrilled the nation with their 175-day flight in 1924. By 1929 the German *Graf Zeppelin* shortened the journey to 21 days, but it was Wiley Post who astounded everyone in 1933 when he soloed the world in less than eight with his Lockheed Vega *Winnie Mae*.

Altitude flying was always a challenge—many marveled when the Wrights reached 360 feet in 1908, but within two years, Ralph Johnstone flew his Wright roadster above 9,000 feet. By 1919, the altitude reached was more than tripled by Roland Rohlfs flying his Curtiss triplane to 31,420 feet. Then Wiley Post claimed another new record in 1934 by flying the *Winnie Mae* to 48,000 feet and into the stratosphere.

Wiley Post with his pressured suit

Although the distance fliers and altitude seekers made headlines, it was the speed demons who brought out the crowds. Glenn Curtiss thrilled the masses when he flew his pusher biplane nearly 46 mph to capture the Gordon Bennett Cup in 1909. Then Major C.S. Mosely upped the record to 178 mph in 1920 to win the first Pulitzer landplane race. By 1925 speed had increased to 233 mph when Lt. James Doolittle won the Schneider Trophy Race for seaplanes. From then on, the air races became the crowd pleasers with big prizes and the screaming whine of streamlined flying machines engaging the masses. By the end of the 1920s, the public's interest convinced aircraft manufacturers that it was to their advantage to create more and better airplanes. This led to the introduction of the Thompson Trophy Race in 1930 and the Bendix Race the following year to showcase the Golden Age of Air Racing—America's best pilots competing each year for hugh cash rewards at the Nationals. But with the speed came more crashes, maiming, and deaths with appalling regularity. But now things were different; there was no mass outcry for change, for races were supported by big business. The aviation industry was growing by leaps and bounds, and no one wanted to slow it down. Building the best racers meant lucrative contracts and big money meant big promotions. The crowds packed in for the same reason that Lincoln Beachey had called them "a pack of jackals"—they thirsted for excitement and lusted for blood. Racing wasn't enough to supply all of that, so there came the rebirth of the air show to add more thrills and excitement. With new machines and more powerful screaming engines, a new generation of stunters, wingwalkers, and jumpers took to the circuit to entertain the crowds. Groups like the Flying Aces, with their high standards of showmanship, carried on well into the 1930s to thrill the spectators and keep the Golden Age of Aviation healthy and alive.....

King of the Daredevils

Ormer Locklear led a far different life from the scores of barnstormers who were to follow him into the air. He earned thousands of dollars a day, stayed in fancy hotels, performed for vast crowds around the nation, and became an international celebrity.

Locklear made his mark shortly after enlisting in the Army Air Service in the fall of 1917 by climbing out of the cockpit of a Curtiss *Jenny* flown by a fellow officer. From his first simple walk on the lower wing among the struts and wires, he soon contrived more hair-raising aerial acrobatics. He loved to stand erect on the *Jenny's* top wing, leaning into the wind to maintain a precarious balance, cutting a dashing figure in his riding boots with their slippery leather soles. It wasn't long before he was changing planes in mid-air, hanging by his hands from the landing gear of one *Jenny* and letting go to sprawl on the upper wing of another.

Locklear and his two compatriot pilots, Milton 'Skeets' Elliott and James Frew, were risking court-martial, as stunting was strictly prohibited. But many cadets were dying in accidents, so the commanding officer decided to utilize Locklear's talents to restore the morale of student pilots by convincing them that the *Jenny* biplane was not necessarily an instrument of death.

After the Armistice, Locklear stayed in the service to refine his reckless stunts with Elliott and 'Shorty' Short who replaced Frew after he returned to civilian life. The trio's new repertoire included Locklear, sans parachute, hopping from the wingtip of one plane to another as the two pilots labored to keep their ships flying evenly side by side.

A chance meeting with fast-talking promoter Bill Pickens in the spring of 1919 convinced Locklear and his pals to resign from the service and get into show business.

Pickens, who considered himself the world's greatest practitioner of the art of ballyhoo, had sensationalized the careers of barnstormer Lincoln Beachey, racecar driver Barney Oldfield, and female parachutist Tiny Broadwick. Now he sensed that he had a hot new property. He did a masterful job of promotion, especially when he was getting 50% of the profits. The trio's first performance drew a crowd of 10,000 to dazzle. And dazzle they did. They were an overnight success, and requests for their services came pouring in. Pickens did not delay in warning Locklear that the public would soon tire of the act unless new, more sensational gimmicks were developed. At Erie, Pennsylvania, Locklear responded with a stunt they hadn't even rehearsed. Standing in an automobile being driven around the exhibition track, he grabbed a ladder slung under Elliot's *Jenny*. Immediately, he was yanked over the windshield and dragged along the ground. With the warm air, the plane was unable to rise with his weight on the ladder. To prevent a crash he let go and spectacularly tumbled along the track. He miraculously escaped serious injury, and was performing again within a couple of days. He worried about the impression of performing with bandages, but Pickens exclaimed, "Bandages are box office, and don't ever forget that we're both capitalizing on sudden death!"

He had set Locklear's minimum price at $1,000, but he worried about how long his client would last, so he decided to sell him to the movies while the selling was good. Hollywood was mad about aviation; Locklear became its darling. Universal Films announced, "For a huge sum, Lieutenant Locklear has agreed to appear in the leading role of a six-reel feature in which will be interpolated all of his amazing feats of acrobatics."

Within days he was diving his *Jenny* on motion-picture lots, running the wheels over the curved roofs of the studio buildings, and wingwalking to the thrill of everyone below.

In the ***Great Air Robbery***, Locklear was called on to scramble up a rope ladder from one plane to another to save a drunken fellow pilot, repeat the stunt to rescue the heroine, then hang from the landing gear of a plane and drop into a speeding automobile, beat up a crook, grab the heroine's jewels, and get back into the plane by way of the landing gear, just as the car went out of control and crashed.

These feats set the stage for new daring in aerial exhibitions, and Pickens didn't miss a beat. Always on the lookout to pocket some more agent fees, he lost no time in booking the aerial team to barnstorm the nation, performing at 22 air shows and fairs in 15 states from August to November of 1919. The constant strain of stunting began to take its toll. Accidents in Illinois and California left Locklear battered and bloody. Although a growing awareness of his mortality and a preoccupation with death was beginning to consume him, he figured with his growing fame he could soon quit the barnstorming circuit and devote himself solely to acting.

His spirits were brightened in April of 1920 when Fox Studios offered him $1,650 a week to appear in a new thriller, ***The Skywayman***. In addition to his normal feats of daring, the final scene was to be the most dangerous stunt ever filmed. For the dramatic night scene finale in which Locklear was to spin to earth from 2,000 feet, the studio planned to combine footage of a model airplane with special effects photography to lessen the risk to their star. But Locklear would have no part of any fakery; his audience would have the real thing. Against their better judgement, the Fox executives finally gave in.

The *Jenny*, having been painted white to make it more visible against the night sky, was ready for the shoot. Five 100,000-candle power arc lights had been positioned, aimed upward, in a semi-circle around the field to cast a pool of peripheral illumination in which the plane could be seen, and to provide Locklear with vertical reference before he ignited magnesium flares on his wings to simulate a flaming crash.

Just before take off, he muttered something about a premonition of not flying that night, but then roared off and disappeared into the darkness with Elliott.

At 3,000 feet, the *Jenny* came into the beam of arc lights. Locklear looped and rolled the plane for 15 minutes, and then, igniting the flares on the wingtips, prompting an admiring outcry from the crowd, dove 2,000 feet before pulling up in a stall and then spinning counter-clockwise toward the ground. His audience watched in fascinated silence, but as he reached 500 feet, someone began to scream, "Cut the lights! Cut the lights!" which appeared to be blinding him. Instead, the arcs began swinging toward the plane, and one by one, trapped it in their shafts of light.

The brilliantly illuminated white *Jenny* went into a vertical dive at 300 feet and plummeted to earth. The sound of the engine ceased. An explosion followed. Then a bright fiery glow lit up the sky.

Few Americans ever went to their graves amid such clamor as did Ormer Locklear. News headlines emblazoned his name from coast to coast. His casket and Elliott's were escorted to the Los Angeles railroad station by a police band, followed by a military honor guard, a troupe of movie cowboys, and a long line of automobiles. As a squadron of airplanes circled overhead, tens of thousands of mourners lined the pathway to pay last respects to their Hollywood star.

Ormer Locklear was placed aboard the train for Fort Worth where fifty thousand people lined the streets to watch his funeral cortege pass in review. Twenty thousand more gathered around the church where services were held, and fifteen thousand came to the cemetery where he was laid to rest.

Though his film career lasted only sixteen months, his talent and daring set the stage for aerial stunting in Hollywood for the years to come.

Innovator in the Sky

He must have been born with flying in his blood, for as a lad of ten, seeing Lincoln Beachey piloting his powered dirigible and thrilling the crowds at the 1905 Lewis and Clark Exposition, Danny Grecco could think of nothing else. He wasted little time in trying to set the aviation world afire by constructing a 15-foot high tissue paper balloon and filling it with hot air by soaking a double handful of waste in kerosene, placing it in a pan at the opening of the balloon, and touching a match to it. As the hot air filled the balloon it took off in a ball of flame, drifting on the wind, with Danny in hot pursuit on his bicycle.

After setting fire to vacant fields and two roof tops in south Portland, and receiving severe reprimands from his parents, Danny ended this project, but not his desire to learn everything he could about flying. His attention was turned to less exciting, but also a less incendiary hobby of building model airplanes. In February of 1912 he won the Meier & Frank model contest with his Curtiss Pusher. This led to the real thing when he helped put the plane together for Silas Christoffersen's renown flight off the roof of Portland's Multnomah Hotel during the 1912 Rose City Festival. The next year he managed to get his first plane ride with Christoffersen aboard a Curtiss-Parker hydroplane. From that moment on, Danny knew that flying was for him. He quit high school and peddled papers to save money for buying a 50-hp water-cooled engine to incorporate into his home-built monoplane, which he flew for the first time in 1915. He had such little control that he was glad when he landed safely. This brief stint of uncontrollable flight made him realize that he had far more to learn if he was going to live to old age. Then came WWI, so he joined the Army Signal Corps as a mechanic to get some more experience.

After the Armistice, Danny was out of a job and needed money, so he decided to get it the easy way, barnstorming the countryside. He soloed in an old *Jenny* in 1918, the day before his 23rd birthday. It wasn't long before he bought this plane and some others to begin five years of stunting and parachute jumping to thrill the crowds at fairs and festivals around the Northwest.

His first parachute jump was over the amusement park at Lotus Isle on the Columbia River. Pioneer parachutist Frank Miller packed Danny's chute into a bundle and tied it to the wing of a *Jenny*. All that Danny had to do was hang on until the plane was high enough, and then fall off the wing and hope that his weight would drag the chute out behind him. He landed without problem, but, of all the stunts he performed, he figured that parachuting was the most dangerous, as any miscalculation while jumping over the river's edge could send him to a watery grave. He did get dunked a few times, but was lucky to escape with only a soaking. Probably his closest shave was the time he was wing walking with Jack Rand piloting at the Tillamook County Fair. Jack put the old *Jenny* into a loop and miscalculated his elevation, so while pulling out he wiped out a pig pen. It amazed Danny that they survived that episode, let alone without a scratch.

Each year the crowds at Columbia Beach became more and more demanding. Simple stunts that once thrilled them were now commonplace, and the aerial entertainers had to be innovative to keep the throngs coming back. Danny Grecco was one of the best of the innovators, and one particular stunt topped them all, for it was all over town about the crazy pilot who was going to drop live turkeys to the crowd over the Labor Day weekend.

About 3,000 persons were gathered at the amusement park awaiting the advertised spectacle when Grecco suddenly changed his mind about following the plan of conducting a "turkey shower". He was threatened with immediate arrest upon the order of Mrs. Frank Swanton, president of the Oregon Humane Society.

All week long protests had been pouring in and Mrs. Swanton exclaimed, "Not only will I arrest Grecco, but all those connected with the resort management." This latter threat clinched the matter. The park management announced that it would cheerfully comply with the Humane Society's order in regard to the turkeys, even though Grecco insisted that the birds could fly and would be harnessed to miniature parachutes.

At the urging of the park management, and not to dissappoint the waiting crowd, Grecco revised his plans and substituted *dead* prizes for air distribution, thus ending the Labor Day escapade.

After the turkey episode Grecco had to become even more innovative to thrill and hold the crowds: he started earning his money by performing death-defying stunts in the air. At every performance, hardly had the plane gotten into the air before the wiry little ex-serviceman clammered to the top wing and took a seat where he rode jauntily until the plane was 1,000 feet in the air. Then, for more than 20 minutes, as the pilot circled high above the crowd, Danny, with the quickness and sureness of a monkey and the daring of a fighter, swung through the maze of wires and spars in such a manner that the watchers below gasped in disbelief. Some of his most incredible stunts involved performing handstands on the top wing and transferring from one aircraft to another in mid-air. What is more amazing is that all the while he was battling an 80-mph wind and working without a parachute. He was absolutely fearless. The finale of the aerial exhibition found Danny perched precariously on the top wing, necks craning in the crowd below, as the plane passed overhead. But it was not until pilot William Graham set his machine spinning like a top as it headed straight for the sandy beach that the spectators made a dash for nowhere in particular, thinking that the machine was never going to come out of its plunge. And all the while Grecco was sitting there waving to everyone in sight.

Danny was known all over the Northwest for these death-defying stunts, but he was in seventh heaven when he was flying his favorite Great Lakes biplane. In it he could perform any stunt in the book. He thrilled audiences with a repertoire of barrel rolls, Immelman turns, loops, and tailspins. He just loved to fly, and continued performing his daredevil stunts through the summer of 1924. That's when the love bug bit him and he started thinking about a safer life after marrying his fiancée, Genevieve. He finally settled down, but never did get flying out of his blood and went on to become one of the best aviation mechanics in the business.

Flight of the Lone Eagle

On May 22, 1919, Raymond Orteig, a New York hotel owner, offered a $25,000 prize to "...the first aviator who shall cross the Atlantic in a land or water aircraft from Paris or the shores of France to New York, or from New York to Paris or the shores of France, without stop."

For years the prize went unclaimed because there simply did not exist an aircraft engine reliable enough to permit a flight of that duration and distance. That is, not until 1926 when Charles Lawrence of the Wright Aeronautical Company designed the 220-hp, air-cooled Wright Whirlwind engine. Almost overnight, speed, endurance, and distance records began falling right and left, but no one had been able to make the 3,300 mile non-stop transatlantic flight. That didn't mean that no one was trying.....Rene Fonck, France's leading World War I ace, had attempted the flight in a heavily loaded Sikorsky trimotor, when the landing gear gave way on take-off from Long Island's Roosevelt Field and two of his crew members perished in the fiery crash. Tony Fokker was building a trimotor for Comdr. Richard E. Byrd to challenge the ocean. The Columbia Aircraft Company was preparing one of Giusepe Bellanca's Wright-powered monoplanes for an attempt. And the U.S. Navy, not to be left out, was readying *The American Legion*, a large Keystone Pathfinder biplane for Lt. Comdr. Noel Davis and Lt. Stanton Wooster to fly. Meanwhile on the other side of the Atlantic, French war hero Capt. Charles Nungesser and Lt. Francois Coli were preparing a French-built Levasseur biplane for an east-west crossing.

One other contender was Charles Lindbergh, a relatively unknown young pilot flying the U.S. Air Mail. It suddenly occurred to him one night while he was on the St. Louis-Chicago run: why couldn't he try the transatlantic flight himself? He had more than four years of aviation behind him, close to two thousand hours in the air, he had barnstormed over half of the nation, and had flown through some of the worst weather the heavens had to offer. Flying experience he had, but not the money, so with $2,000 of his own savings he approached a group of St. Louis business men to convince them that such a flight was possible. And if they agreed to supply $13,000 toward the purchase of a monoplane equipped with one of the new Wright engines, he would personally oversee the project as well as make the flight.

They immediately questioned the safety of attempting such a journey in a single-engine plane, but Lindbergh countered that the more engines a plane had, the more chances there were for an engine failure. Also, he argued, the more engines the more expensive the machine. Realizing that he and his backers could not afford any of the planes manufactured by major companies, he recommended an aircraft built by the relatively unknown Ryan Airlines of San Diego.

They finally agreed to his proposal. Without delay, he was off to California, and on February 24th he wired back that Ryan would build a plane complete with the Whirlwind engine and standard instruments for $10,500, within sixty days.

Sixty days after the deal was closed, the *Spirit of St. Louis* was ready to fly. No radio or sextant was included, for he figured he would rely on dead reckoning for navigation. The weight he saved would mean that he could carry more fuel, so the tank capacity was increased to 425 gallons. In his mind, extra fuel was his greatest reserve for success, but the race for the Orteig prize was becoming close, and the required sixty-day rule between a pilot's entry application and his flight meant that Lindbergh couldn't take off before the end of May.

On April 16th, Commander Byrd and his crew were test flying their trimotor Fokker at Hasbrouck Height, New Jersey. The overweight plane made a successful landing, but hit a soft spot on the field, causing the ship to nose over, injuring all but one of the crew.

Then on April 24th, Clarence Chamberlain took his Wright-Bellanca for a spin, lost a wheel during landing, and severely damaged the plane.

On April 26th, Lieutenant Commander Davis and Lieutenant Wooster were killed while on their last trial run when their Keystone Pathfinder crashed into a marsh short of landing at Langley Field.

On May 8th, Nungesser and Coli took off from La Bourget field near Paris and headed over the North Atlantic for New York. They were never heard from again.

By now the New York-Paris flight was becoming the news story of the year: four men were dead, three injured, and two missing. Byrd and Chamberlain had their planes repaired and ready to go, awaiting suitable weather. By now the *Spirit of St. Louis* was ready to fly, and Lindbergh tested her by flying from San Diego to New York, with one stop in St. Louis. Arriving at Long Island on May 12th, he set a new transcontinental record of 14 hours and 25 minutes. Like his competitors, he found himself weatherbound.

Late in the afternoon of May 19th, he received a special report from the New York Weather Bureau. A high-pressure area was over the entire North Atlantic, the fog was predicted to lift, and there were no more storms in the forecast. Lindy was the only contender completely ready to take advantage of the prospective weather break. That evening he went to Curtiss Field to get the ship ready. On the way he bought five ham and chicken sandwiches to take with him on the flight. These, along with five cans of Army emergency rations and four quarts of water were to be his total supply of food and drink. He loaded in a small air raft, a hunting knife, some cord and twine, a needle, flashlight, hack saw blade, four flares, and a tube of matches. After that he headed back to his hotel for a couple of hours of sleep.

Getting some rest was out of the question. Additional departure details made it clearly impossible, and just before dawn he headed back toward the field.

Spirit
of
t.Louis.

The news leaked out the night before that an early-morning flight across the Atlantic was imminent. In the cold rainy hours after midnight, thousands of cars moved along the roads to Long Island. By the time Lindbergh was ready to return there, all of the roads to Curtiss Field were filled with one-way traffic, and a police escort was needed to bring him through. The crowd wouldn't let up, and followed as the *Spirit of St. Louis* was towed from Curtiss to Roosevelt Field.

At the first light of dawn the rain stopped. The plane was fueled, and at 7:40 A.M. the engine was warmed. At 7:52 Lindy started down the east-west runway. Heavily loaded with fuel, the Ryan bumped twice before she was air-borne. After clearing a tractor at the end of the runway, a telephone wire, and then some tall trees on a hill, Lindy and his plane were headed over Long Island Sound.

The haze lifted, and the three-hundred mile run from Cape Cod to Nova Scotia was clear. Then he ran into occasional cloudbursts.

After leaving the Newfoundland shoreline, he took to the open sea. Hour after hour over the North Atlantic—nothing but water and an occasional iceberg.

Late in the day, fog began rolling in and rising in height. By 10:00 P.M. that night Lindy was flying at 10,000 feet to skim over the clouds. He tried going through a high accumulation, but ice collecting on the plane forced him to immediately seek clear skies. After moonrise, flying was easier, and the danger of sleepiness diminished. Flying eastward, dawn came for him around 1:00 A.M. New York time.

As the sun warmed the air, the fog began to dissipate, so he dropped to a few hundred feet above the water to fly in the clear air. That was short-lived, for after a few miles he faced two hours of complete whiteout.

Then as the fog lifted, Lindy dropped closer to the whitecapped water. During the early part of the day he saw porpoises playing and a few birds, but no sign of human activity. Toward evening he spotted a small fishing boat a bit south of his course, and shortly, more came into view. Within an hour the outline of a rugged coast appeared on the horizon. Flying on, he located Cape Valentia and Dingle Bay on the isle of Ireland. From then on there was almost always a ship in sight. Within two hours he was over England and heading for the Channel. After the sun set, the beacons of the London-Paris airway guided his way, and at 10:00 P.M., European time, he could see the lights of Paris emblazoning the sky. It wasn't long before he was circling the Eiffel Tower. Then spotting the lights from Le Bourget airfield, he continued to circle overhead until he could see hangars at the edge of the field. Then he saw that the roads were jam packed with automobiles. It appeared that all of Paris had turned out to see him land.

And in fact they had, for as soon as word flashed that the *Spirit of St. Louis* was sighted over Ireland, the citizens of Paris began to swarm to Le Bourget where the landing was scheduled to take place. Reports varied greatly, but the general opinion was that over 120,000 people were there to greet him.

After 33½ hours in the air the plane touched down and the crowd went wild. Lindy and the French officials were completely unprepared for the welcoming. Tens of thousands of men and women broke down fences and rushed past the guards. There was an official reception committee but it was swamped in the flood of humanity. No sooner had Lindy opened the door of the plane than he found himself lying in a prostrate position, on top of the crowd and in the center of an ocean of heads that extended as far into the darkness as he could see. The noise was deafening as thousands of voices mingled into a roar.

He tried hard to get to his feet, but it was impossible. His head and shoulders went down, then up, then down again. It was like drowning in a human sea.

It was only through the efforts of French aviator Detroyat and civilian pilot Delage that he was saved from the frenzied mass of well-wishers. Detroyat managed to grab Lindy's arm and get him to his feet. Then they grabbed his hat and shoved it onto the head of an American reporter, shouting, "Here is Lindbergh! Here is Lindbergh!" As the crowd took out after the hapless reporter, Detroyat manuevered Lindy to the outskirts of the crowd while Delage retrieved his little Renault car for a getaway. Trying to communicate with the French aviators was nearly hopeless, for after the long flight Lindy could hardly hear, he spoke not a word of French and his new friends very little English. He was concerned about his plane, but they assurred him, the best they could, that the *Spirit of St. Louis* was safe. Their main concern was to get him away from the crowd and to safety.

The welcoming he received that night at Le Bourget was only a forerunner of what was to come. For weeks afterward he was greeted by thundering crowds in France, Belgium, England, and America. The entire world would be captivated by this shy, young aviator who overcame formidable odds to finally conquer the Atlantic waters...overnight, he had transformed from a little-known mail pilot into an international hero.

Racing with a Double Jinx

Tex Rankin, one of the greatest aerobatic pilots of all time, was a true showman at heart. Defying superstition, he painted a large number 13 on his Waco biplane racer for the 1927 New York-to-Spokane Air Derby, figuring to get nation-wide publicity, regardless of how well he did in the race. He guessed right, for clear across the nation, he and his ship were photographed and featured by the media more than any other entry in the race.

Then he gained even more notoriety when the plane's engine blew up over Montana. Newspaper headlines blazed across the country: **JINX 13 CATCHES UP WITH TEX RANKIN!** Even though Tex was out of the money, the national publicity didn't hurt his flying business back in Portland, Oregon one bit.

The following year he decided to take his jinx-defying stunt one step further by advertising for a black cat to accompany him during the National Race. On the appointed day about a hundred cat owners showed up at Tex's airfield with their feline pride and joys. From the mass of fur, claws, and fluffed tails, a jet black, part-Siamese named Alba Barba, or *White Whisker*, stood out, and its owner, little Carol Mangold, was persuaded to release her pet to Tex's custody.

Without delay, training was started with several days devoted to breaking Alba Barba into aerial travel.

Then on August 24th, with his flying black cat settled in the front cockpit, and huge number 13s emblazoned on the sides of his ship, Tex took off for New York. To keep the home crew apprized of his progress, Tex decided to send telegrams as he made his way across the country.

The consensus back at the home base was that the cat was going to be nothing but trouble, but when the wires were received from California, New Mexico, Texas, Missouri, Ohio, and New Jersey, all indications were that everything was going fine.

The next word from Tex came on September 4th. It read: **LANDED ROOSEVELT FIELD, LONG ISLAND, NEW YORK, TODAY. SHIPS FROM EVERY STATE IN UNION HERE. SPENT DAY VISITING WITH GANG. SHIP, MOTOR, AND CAT IN FINE CONDITION. TAKE OFF TOMORROW 5 A.M. START OF RACE. WIRE YOU AGAIN TONIGHT. REGARDS, TEX.**

The gang back home was ready to admit to its foolish reservations and concede that the black cat really was good luck. From then on, everyone at Rankin Field grouped around the office every morning to hear the latest on how the race was progressing and how lucky the cat was.

Tex drew number 36 take-off position from Roosevelt Field, but by the time he reached Columbus, Ohio on September 6th, he was up to 4th place, with the best time for any plane with an OX-5 engine.

The home crew was ecstatic. If luck held, Tex had a chance to land in the winner's circle at Los Angeles. Then, the September 7 telegram gave the first hint of problems. His engine was acting up during the flight to Kansas City, but after working on it until 1 o'clock in the morning, he made up for it with the fastest time for the Oklahoma City to Fort Worth stretch. The bad news was that someone stole his cat at Kansas City.

A follow-up telephone call from Tex confirmed the loss of his cat, but he also related that Alba Barba had been anything but a jinx: "When I went to get kitty out of the cockpit at Columbus for her sandpile routine, I discovered a gas leak that would have put me out of the race. Had it not been for the cat, I wouldn't have found that leak."

After the loss of his mascot, hard luck seemed to be dogging Tex. Between Fort Worth and Abilene, an oil line broke, causing a delay which slipped him back to fifth place. By El Paso, he had dropped to eighth.

Then on the afternoon of September 8th, good news came to Rankin Field by wire: **FOUND YOUR JINX CAT CAUGHT BY HARNESS IN WEEDS NEAR FLYING FIELD. WHERE WILL I SEND IT? TOM HERRING, KANSAS CITY.**

The gang at Rankin Field was elated—the cat had been located. They immediately telegraphed Tex that the cat had been found. The wire went on to ask if he wanted *Old Blackie* to be sent to Portland or shipped directly to him in Los Angeles.

Tex's answer was received early the next morning: **HAVE CAT SHIPPED TO ME IN LOS ANGELES CARE OF AMERICAN AIRCRAFT CORPORATION. DO NOT INTEND FLYING HOME WITHOUT MY MASCOT. VERY LITTLE CHANCE OF GETTING FOURTH PLACE. REGARDS TEX.**

By the time Tex reached Los Angeles, Walt Bohrer and Dean Goodwin had arrived from Portland, picked up the cat, and were waiting at Mines Field to greet him.

Tex was the third pilot to arrive in Los Angeles, but his elapse time gave him the fifth place standing, good enough to be in the money, but he was anxious to get back to Portland. Dusk was closing in fast so he gave his long-time employee, Walt Bohrer, the job of cat-sitting on the trip home. With the cat leashed to the spare magnito Tex kept in the front cockpit, Walt settled himself next to the suspicious feline. Just before takeoff, Tex handed Walt a flashlight. "What's this for?" Walt asked.

"Well," Tex said, "when we get over those Tehachipi Mountains, its gonna be mighty dark. I want you to shine that light around so we won't hit any of those 6,000-foot peaks! I want to get to Bakersfield tonight to listen to the Hoover-Smith election returns."

By the time they reached the rugged Tehachapis, they were flying in total darkness, and Tex yelled to Walt to shine the light to see how well they were clearing the trees. As ludicrous as it sounds, Walt leaned over the side of the cockpit to shine the flashlights 1,000-foot beam from right to left, as if it would prevent them from hitting a peak if one suddenly appeared in the light, when all of a sudden they hit a downdraft and out went the cat!

By the time Walt managed to get the flashlight back into the cockpit, the cat's harness had all but slipped over her head. Anchored to the heavy mag, the cat hung halfway between the cockpit and the lower wing, and her nine lives were being used up pretty quickly. It was a good thing she had a tail, because that is all that saved her from falling to eternity, for nothing else was in reach for Walt to grab. With a painful effort, he was able to get the ball of yowling, clawing fur back into the cockpit.

About that time Tex spotted the welcome green beacon of the Kern County Airport in Bakersfield, and dove the plane in practically wide open.

The following day's flight was uneventful, except that the cat warily eyed Walt the entire time. As they neared Redding however, the plane's faithful OX-5 engine started overheating. The first thing that came to Walt's mind was the Black Cat Jinx! As it turned out, the cat was only to jinx him, for Tex didn't want to cross Siskiyou Mountains of Oregon with too heavy a load, and since Walt far outweighed the cat, he was chosen to finish the trip to Portland by bus, while Tex flew home with his feline companion.

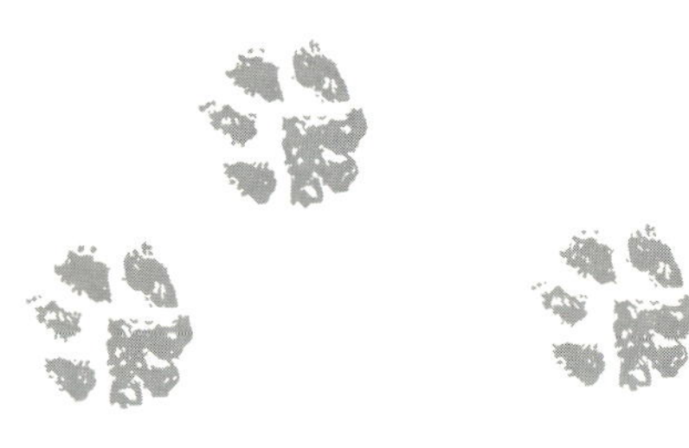

A Red-Letter Day

In order to augment his flying school's coffers, Tex Rankin frequently staged an aerial circus to bring out the crowds in and around the Portland, Oregon area. Since aviation was still in its pioneer stages in the late 1920s, spectators wouldn't dream of missing an exhibition, especially if Tex himself was going to perform his aerobatic maneuvers which never failed to leave the crowd with goose bumps.

For the summer of 1928, Tex planned a real 'red-letter' day: not only would he dazzle the crowd with his trick flying, but they also would be treated to something special—parachute jumping by a dozen-and-a-half students who had signed up to make their first exit from a plane in flight. Tex believed it was a good idea for anyone learning to fly to also go through the experience of making a parachute jump, since someday one of them might be forced to join the exclusive group known as the *Caterpillar Club*, made up of those who were forced to jump from an airplane to save their lives. His pitch was so convincing, that even his secretary, Ann Bohrer, was planning on jumping that day.

The parachute event was scheduled to open the show at one o'clock. But long before that time, hundreds of thrill seekers, anticipating an exciting afternoon of aerial entertainment, had already congregated around the airfield.

Promptly at one o'clock, the students who had signed up to make a jump, gathered around the announcer to see who would be the first to go. Since there were three women in the group, Tex decided that it would be a better attraction to let them precede the men, so with their names in a hat, the announcer pulled out a slip of paper and called out: "Ann 'Halfpint' Bohrer!", followed by her introduction to the crowd as Tex's private secretary and an assignment of a bright red chute to start off the show.

The second name drawn was Faye 'Tiny' Carter, Ann's side-kick in the Rankin office. She was assigned a blue chute. The third name out of the hat was that of Dorothy Hester, who was assigned to bail out with a white parachute.

After all of the introductions were completed, the girls scurried off to don harnesses over their flying togs. Looking on were hundreds of pairs of eyes. The menagerie of expressions ran the gamut—surprise, admiration, awe, curiosity, and just plain disgust at such folly.

As Ann worked her way through the crowd, she could see Frank Brooks, who was a world champion parachutist, busily folding a large exhibition chute. A broad grin spread over his face as she stepped up, for he remembered only a few days before, her strong refusal to ever consider jumping from a plane. His grin spread to outright laughter as he took full advantage of the situation—all to the expense and embarrassment of Ann. Several bystanders seemed to get caught up in the moment and joined in the teasing. Some said that the harness didn't look very strong, and others said they had noticed a rip in the chute while Brooks was folding it.

Finally the job was done, and after some brief instructions on how to climb out on the wing, where to hold on, how to step off the wing, and how to land on the ground, Ann was approached by a photographer who asked if she would kindly step on the wing of the plane for a picture. Amid shouts from the crowd encouraging her to "smile", she finally heard the camera shutter click. Then she climbed into the cockpit. Brooks attached the brilliant red 28-foot parachute to her harness, climbed aboard, and Tex taxied his Waco-10 biplane onto the runway as Ann waved back at the crowd of spectators.

As Tex took off and climbed for elevation, Ann's nerves had settled down, and her only sensation was an acute eagerness to make the jump.

After flying about for some time to gain final elevation and test the air currents and wind direction, Tex turned the plane in the general direction of the field and began stalling the ship. As Ann looked over the edge of the cockpit at the vast panorama, she began to have second thoughts about what she was doing, but a loud voice brought her back to attention. It was Tex telling her to climb on the wing. Without thinking, she was over the edge of the cockpit and grasping a strut for support. Brooks knelt on the seat and steadied the chute while Tex braced her back with one hand. She slowly wormed her way back to the trailing edge of the wing until her heels extended over the wing's edge and her hands grasped the edge of the rear cockpit. There she was, leaning out in space for what seemed an eternity as Tex continued circling to further check the wind to be sure she would land in the center of the field.

Every little bit, Tex would smile reassuringly at Ann. He had instructed her not to be frightened: "Just push yourself backwards away from the ship and let go when we tell you to, so watch our lips!" Suddenly Brooks lips began to move, Ann tensed, ready to push off, then hesitated; he was only licking his dry lips. After a few more false signals, Brooks finally mouthed, "Now! Go!" Ann instinctively obeyed and pushed away from the ship and stepped backwards.

Down—down—down, feet first, then flat on her back, now head dropping. Her eyes closed in spite of her resolve to keep them fastened on the ship. Everything went blank for a second. Then she opened them to see her booted feet, and beyond them, twisted shroud lines and a thin streamer of parachute following as she plummeted earthward. The plane was no longer in sight, and the parachute gave no indication of opening. It didn't occur to her that in the folding, the lines might have somehow become fouled, for there was never any question of Brook's competence as a parachute rigger—he had been in the business for 25 years.

But now she was beginning to wonder as she hurtled through space. Then the chute was slowly filling at the top—how thrilling to watch! When suddenly, Purfrf! it opened with a vengeance, jerking Ann into an upright position. As the fouled lines unwound, her small body twisted violently around, first in one direction and then the other, before the lines finally straightened. Looking up, she remarked to herself how pretty her red chute looked in the sunlight; looking straight down she was happy to see that the ground was no longer rushing up at her. In fact, she seemed to be going up instead of down!

"They should have given me a smaller parachute," she thought belatedly. With her weight of 95 pounds, the chute was taking her away from the field and over a myriad of lakes and ponds toward the Columbia River. For the first time, a sudden fear came over her—she was afraid of water and didn't know how to swim, but it wouldn't have helped her anyway, since her boots and heavy parachute were bound to drag her below the surface. All she could do was to thrill to the exhilarating experience as she floated in space. Looking down again, the earth seemed closer; in fact, it was coming up very fast. She was relieved to know that she was actually going to land, though it was nowhere near the airfield. She had drifted nearly a mile from the intended drop spot, right over a pasture full of cattle and into a stand of willows and alders. Instinctively, at the last moment, she threw her arms across her face for protection.

In spite of the instructions and pointers on landing, she had absolutely no control of the situation and landed smack on her face headlong across a bunch of twigs which covered a small ditch. Floating above her was her bright red chute which drifted down to rest over the trees. Lying there on her stomach, with her face buried in the twigs, moss, and leaves, she was glad that no one had witnessed her undignified landing. But she wasn't hurt, and scrambling to her feet she was able to recover in time to signal to the plane overhead that she was O.K.. The only problem was that the chute was hung up in the trees and she would have to wait for help from the field. The waiting seemed like hours, but it wasn't long before her rescuers arrived and they were struggling through the brush, over ditches, and across pastures on their way back to the airfield. Finally, a pickup truck caught up with them for transportation the rest of the way to the field where a crowd of over 8,000 spectators welcomed them with a rousing cheer. For the second time that day, Ann was introduced with flowery words and given enthusiastic applause. It was then that she learned the Brooks had somehow mispacked the chute, causing her to fall over 2,500 feet before the canopy opened. Tex and Brooks also worried that the chute may have broken her back when the opening jerked her upright, or that being spun so viciously by the lines may have broken her neck. Needless to say everyone was greatly relieved when she returned without a scratch.

While Ann was waiting to be found, Faye Carter, the next in line, made her jump. She did somewhat better because she landed closer to the field. However, she and her parachute came to rest on top of the telephone wires that ran adjacent to the airstrip, and it took the local fire department to rescue her. By then Tex and Brooks must have had the wind drift figured out, for Dorothy Hester, the third woman to jump, came down smack-dab in the center of the field to the thunderous applause of the spectators.

The rest of the jumping went off without a hitch, and Tex ended the program with his usual dazzle, but it was the girls who won the hearts of the crowd that day.

Topless in the Sky

It is difficult to figure out how young Jessie Schultz got involved with a pilot. She didn't even like airplanes, and couldn't see any future at all in the dirty, noisy, miserable things. But, too, neither could she see any future for an active young girl of nineteen in Ulysses, Kansas. She'd had her fill of the open prairie while growing up and working on the family wheat farm near Seward.

She was ten years old when her father leased the farm and moved the family out to Olympia, Washington, but after finishing her second year of college at Washington State, here she was, back in Kansas. It was to be only a summer visit, but her father had some kind of land deal going and decided to stay, telling her, "There are lots of colleges in Kansas for you to go to."

Jessie let out a bawl, "I'm not going to any old cow college." Not only was she heartbroken, she was mad. This little town was right out in the country with only a handful of people. She had been active all of her life, playing in the band, teaching violin lessons, and participating in athletics: on the go all the time. There couldn't be anything worse for a nineteen-year-old girl than to be buried in a Kansas cow town. She was so utterly disgusted that she would do anything to get out of there.

Then one day her little brother called to her. "There is someone out in the pasture asking for you."

Outside Jessie met Jimmie Woods. He was looking for someone to wash his airplane. Of course, he probably had an ulterior motive, as single young girls weren't very plentiful in Ulysses. And single men probably weren't either. Anyway, Jessie figured washing airplanes was a whole lot better than chasing after a bunch of cows.

By the end of summer, Jimmie planned to leave the place because he was starving to death, and told her, "If you want to go, fine! It's up to you."

Now Jessie's father had no use for Jimmie Woods. He was 31 years old, spent all of his time with planes, and wasn't making a good living with his garage business. But Jessie, like most teenagers, was in high revolt, and this was her chance to escape. She knew her dad would never permit her leaving, so she had to come up with a deceptive scheme.

Throughout the summer, whenever she had a date with Jimmie, a couple that were friends had to call on her so she could meet on the sly. So that's how she planned her getaway. The couple showed up at the door and called on Jessie to get her violin to play for a dance in the next town, saying that she could stay with them that night. Jessie lost no time in packing a small valise with her toothbrush, pajamas, three $50 baby bonds from World War I, and a few other items. Then she picked up her violin case and left the house, heading for the justice of the peace in the next town.

Jimmie and his brother had sold their farmland and garage to pay off their airplanes. They figured to head South for the winter, so after the ceremony, the newlyweds and Jimmie's brother flew off to Wichita for the honeymoon, and then went to barnstorming, with Jessie selling tickets for $1.00 a head to bring in some cash. The price wasn't much, but these were troubled times, and a dollar went a long way for some poor soul feeding a family. Their business got so bad that they decided to tie in with two other pilots so they could make more of a splash, but that meant more mouths to feed and expenses to meet.

Jessie was miserable. This was the first time she had gone hungry in her life, and sometimes it would be days with little or nothing to eat. On top of that, their bed was sleeping outdoors with only the wings of the plane for cover.

One day the fellows were sitting around shooting off their mouths. One of the guys remarked, "What we need is an attraction to bring people out here, and hold them so we can sell some tickets. What we need is a wingwalker. Yah! We need a woman wingwalker."

Simultaneously, they all turned and stared at Jessie. Then they started slicktalking her until she gave in. All the guys had heard of wingwalking but none of them had any idea of how to do it. Right away, Jessie started having second thoughts: for someone who didn't like airplanes, why would she want to walk that close to death?

They started on the ground, with their new star practicing walking along the front edge of the wing. It wasn't long before they felt confident enough to try working in the air. But Jimmie didn't want to take any chance of losing his new bride, so he took a tie-down rope and wrapped it around her waist, fastening it securely with a big knot. Then he tied the other end to the plane so she wouldn't go very far if she did happen to fall.

With Jessie settled in the front cockpit, they were ready for takeoff. Jimmie revved the engine of his OX-5 Swallow and taxied out onto the field and lifted off. As soon as they were high in the air, he throttled back to slow the craft and yelled at Jessie to scram. She had never had her head out of the cockpit before, and as she stood up she was hit with the wind. Suddenly her mouth went dry. She knew right then and there that she was living the last moments of her life. She was no chicken, but she had never been so utterly frightened in her life; she truly thought she was about to die.

Getting a real rush from the prop blast, Jessie finally mustered enough courage to step out onto the walkway and start working her way forward. Flying along at 85 miles an hour, one false step to eternity, her fear wasn't lessening a bit. As she climbed through the maze of wires the trailing rope hung up; now, she also had to contend with the rope entanglement. Working her way loose, she struggled back to the cockpit, at which point her fear turned to anger.

Up to that point she had been the silent partner of the marriage, but as soon as the plane was on the ground she let Jimmie have a piece of her mind. If she was going to be the wingwalker, she wasn't going to be hampered by any old safety line.

The only time she relented to a rope was to have one fastened to the center section of the top wing so she could ride it like a surfboard, sitting on the leading edge while tucking her toes under the wires and hanging onto it while Jimmie performed spins, loops, and rolls. It was a real crowd pleaser, but a tough way to eke out a living.

Worst of all was the competition. A lot of fly-by-night outfits were on the circuit, collecting their money and then flying off without paying their bills, giving all of the flying groups a bad name. To get away from the stigma, Jimmie and Jessie spruced up the act, got some uniforms, and started calling the group the ***Flying Aces***. They began working with organizations to sell the tickets and collect the money. That way they could concentrate on the performance. Jessie started parachuting and working with a rope ladder. The stunts were getting more spectacular, and business was getting better. By the fall of 1929, the Flying Aces averaged at least 52 shows a year, working from the Atlantic seaboard to the Rocky Mountains and from the Canadian border into Mexico, before laying off for the winter. It wasn't long before they had a crew of 14-15, 5 airplanes, a sound system, advance man, and all of their own support equipment. Their only need was a coordinator to work with and a place to do the show.

Between shows, Jessie always got the job of ferrying their little Cub plane from town to town. The long trips were pretty lonely so, for company, she got herself a bulldog. Named Chandelle, she became Jessie's faithful companion while she spent long hours in the air.

On the circuit, Jessie went by the name of *Miss Jessie Martin*. This was show business, and it was more of an attraction than for her to be announced as Mrs. Jimmy Woods.

Besides wingwalking and parachuting, her rope ladder act was a real crowd pleaser, and one day it turned out to be super spectacular. Dressed in white slacks and shirt, she was just completing her act, hanging upside down from the end of the ladder when the wind started her shirt to billowing. Suddenly the buttons started popping off, and the next thing she knew the wind had split the shirt right down the back. Patches of cloth started trailing off, then the shirt completely disintegrated. Next to go was her brassiere. There she was, in the most precarious predicament with her brassiere flapping in the wind; Jessie could do nothing except use her arms to stay decent while hanging onto the ladder for dear life.

By this time Bobby Gunn, the pilot, was wondering what was wrong. Jessie should have been finished with her act and back in the cockpit by now. Just then he saw her head appear. One arm came up and all he could see was bare skin. Then her other arm came into view, and there was more bare skin. Being young and bashful, he ducked down in the rear cockpit just as Jessie climbed into the front section. She was safely out of view at last, but another problem faced her when they landed. She would have to get out in front of the crowd, and there was nothing available to cover her. Bobby came to the rescue by taking his shirt off and passing it over the windshield for her to put on.

Covered back to decency, Jessie breathed a sigh of relief, thinking that the spectators on the ground couldn't see well enough to realize what had really happened.

A few minutes later they landed and taxied up to the crowd. As Jessie climbed out, a male spectator stepped forward. There is always a smart aleck in every crowd and there he stood, waving a fancy telescope in the air while remarking in a booming voice, "Miss Martin, I want to tell you how much I thoroughly enjoyed your act up there."

Dealt a Bad Hand by Fate

Despite all of the hazards of barnstorming across the country, the ***Flying Aces*** maintained a remarkable safety record. Jimmy Woods and his wife Jessie hired all of their own pilots; that way they could keep control, making sure that each showed up sober and on time for performances. Also, Jimmy did all of his own inspecting. As a master mechanic, he made sure that his fleet of aircraft was always maintained and in perfect flying condition.

One summer day they were barnstorming their way westward, and when they reached Colorado, a young fellow showed up looking for a flying job. They didn't need any pilots, but they figured they could use some help on the ground, that is, if he was interested.

Sure he was interested! The newcomer was Herb Bassett, a very shy, but rugged bronc rider who wanted more than anything else in the world to fly. He had just finished training at the Colorado Springs Flight School. His mother had taken in sewing to make ends meet, but she did hold out enough money to pay for her son's lessons. Now he was desperate; he would settle for any kind of work, as long as it was around airplanes.

Herb proved to be a hard worker, always looking for ways to make some extra cash. Besides being on the ground crew for the Aces, he put his agility to work parachuting during the shows. Then one day he got his big break, a chance to fly during one of the performances. Lilio Venvenuti had shown up with his Eaglerock biplane, planning to make some money by hauling passengers around, but having only a private license, he wasn't allowed to. So Herb took over the Eaglerock, ferrying passengers on short hops around the field. He even got to fill in with the Aces, working the serpentine and performing some simple tricks.

Toward the end of the season, Herb had become pretty much of a regular with the show. One day, filling in with Venvenuti's plane, Herb climbed high above the crowd and began a series of loops and spins. Suddenly, without warning, the top wing of the Eaglerock folded back, right over the open cockpit. From the ground it looked like he was trapped and struggling to get out. Almost immediately the plane went into a spin and started to lose altitude at an alarming rate.

As a last ditch effort to escape the entanglement, Herb stood halfway up in the cockpit and pulled his rip cord. The silk popped out, and as he seemed to have planned, the parachute pulled him away from the wreckage. But the plane was still in a spin and the fuselage whipped around, catching the shroud lines and slapping Herb into its side. There he hung, entirely helpless, with the plane out of control and spinning faster and faster.

There was nothing anyone could do but stare in horror as the entanglement of broken plane, pilot, and chute spun into the ground. Through no fault of his own, but a most tragic accident caused by owner neglect in improperly maintaining his aircraft, Herb Bassett's young life ended. His mangled body was gathered up and shipped back to his loving mother in Colorado.

A few years later, on another show tour through the area, Jessie Woods discovered that someone had built a house across the road from the airfield. In the front yard was a beautiful bush of roses climbing over the tail section of the Eaglerock biplane, planted as a living memorial to the bashful young pilot who lost his life doing what he loved most of all.

Queen of the Stunters

As a young girl of twelve, growing up in Portland, Oregon, Dorothy Hester loved to read tales of great adventure, which led to a burning desire to travel to faraway lands like Arabia or Morocco. Then one day a neighbor riding with Dorothy on a streetcar, asked her if she had ever flown. She said that she hadn't, but that started her thinking of another kind of quest.

Nearly five years passed, and just before her seventeenth birthday, she decided to celebrate with her dream of an airplane ride. After rushing home for some money, she boarded a trolley, then made two transfers before reaching Rankin Field on Swan Island. With the wind gusting through her hair, she was so thrilled with her first plane ride that she knew right then and there that aviation was her ticket to see the world.

But there was a hitch: it cost $250 just to attend ground school, and double that for flight training. That was an awful lot of money to a seventeen-year-old girl, especially since she was making only 32¢ an hour employed at the local woolen mill. But Dorothy was determined. After working all day, she attended evening classes at the Rankin School of Flying, the largest of its kind in the world. Even though the school was turning out some of the best pilots in the world, Tex Rankin wasn't ready to take on any girl for pilot instruction.

That didn't faze Dorothy one bit. She successfully completed ground school, and was eager to start flight training, but the $500 cost dimmed the prospect. As luck would have it, an airshow was scheduled in the town of Medford, and promoters needed something special to attract the crowd and spark the show. What better way to do it than to have a girl parachute from a plane.

With $100 promised for one jump, Dorothy couldn't pass up the opportunity. The next thing she remembered was climbing out of the cockpit of the Waco-9 biplane onto the wing where the life-saving silk was stuffed into a bag.

As the plane reached a safe jumping altitude, Dorothy began having second thoughts of what she was doing. The pilot kept the plane flying in tight circles high above the crowd of thrill seekers; the more he circled, the tighter Dorothy hung on. The patience of the pilot and crowd below began wearing thin, and Dorothy still showed no signs of jumping. Finally out of desperation, the pilot unsnapped the fire extinguisher and began cracking her on the knuckles, causing her to finally let go.

With the wind at her back, and the silken canopy overhead, she was in the air floating gracefully earthward. Now she had time to think: just four more jumps and she would have enough money saved to complete her flight training.

Even when she turned up at the field with cash in her pocket, Tex still didn't think there was any hope for a girl to pilot one of his planes, so he turned her over to his lead instructor Elrey Jeppesen. It didn't take too many flights with Jepp before he could see that this girl had the makings of a great pilot. Eventually, her enthusiasm, skill, and determination changed Tex's attitude. In fact, he was so impressed that he asked her if she would be interested in learning acrobatic flying.

Dorothy was thrilled at the prospect. Right after work she would head to Swan Island to practice loops, spins, rolls, and inverted flying. On weekends she practiced her acrobatics for the locals who came to the field for picnics and entertainment. Now instead of paying for lessons, she was trading her aerial performances for more acrobatic trainings. As Tex's protege she learned feats that no woman had ever tried before, mastering them all with little difficulty.

On June 30, 1930, at the age of nineteen, Dorothy made the record book—the first woman ever to fly a plane in an outside loop. With that accomplishment, Tex knew she was ready for the big-time, and started scheduling for a Northwest Air Tour from Los Angeles to Chicago. All summer and fall were spent refining routines, then in February of 1931 Tex and Dorothy flew to the Grand Central Air Terminal in Glendale, California to start their three-month, thirty-eight state tour.

Flying a Great Lakes biplane powered with a 90-horsepower Cirrus engine, Dorothy warmed up the crowd with her aerobatic repertoire, and then improved on her record by executing five outside loops. The following day Tex added to the excitement by completing seventy-eight outside loops to set a new world's record, but not without toll to himself—the head-long dives under full power of the engine caused his head to spin and nose to bleed for days afterward.

At the Omaha Air Races in mid-May, with a crowd of over 20,000 spectators, Dorothy stole the show—all of the old-time pilots just stood around gaping, amazed at her aerobatic skill. On the 15th she set a world's record for both men and women by completing 56 inverted snap rolls before the plane's fuel supply was exhausted. And then two days later she took a crack at her outside loop record. After two hours and six minutes she had completed 62 outside loops, with no ill effects. To everyone's amazement she came close to matching Tex's record, and she might even have broken it if she hadn't run low on fuel.

Her crowning performance at Omaha brought her star status, being proclaimed the greatest woman aerobatic pilot on earth. This caused the National Air Race officials in Cleveland to break from tradition and invite her to be the first woman to ever perform at the Nationals. Immediately upon her arrival at the show, the Great Lakes Aircraft Corporation presented her with her very own Great Lakes sport trainer, and Dorothy lost little time in giving it a good testing. As thousands of spectators held their breath and stared in fascination, she took command of the air, maneuvering her biplane through a series of 36 death-defying stunts. Besides her outside loops and inverted snap rolls she electrified the crowd with a dozen-and-a-half other stunts while flying upside down.

Then, at one performance, her inverted flying nearly became her undoing. She was in the air, gaining altitude for her exhibition while a tow plane pulling four gliders entertained the crowd below. At the appointed time she started her routine and progressed through a series of skillful maneuvers, ending her act with an inverted spin, in which she was upside down, losing altitude rapidly, and blind to what was going on below. The air was supposed to be clear, but for some unknown reason the tow plane was still pulling the gliders over the field. She spun right through the tangle of plane, tow ropes, and gliders—amazingly missing everything in the air.

It was her ultimate stunt—a once-in-a-lifetime, unplanned, heart-stopping performance that neither she nor anyone else there would ever forget.

Around the World with the Winnie Mae

Even though Wiley Post grew up on farms from Texas to Oklahoma, he never did take to tilling the soil. Along with that he also developed an intense dislike for school, and after age eleven his only interest seemed to be in mechanical devices. That was reaffirmed about three years later when he saw exhibition flyer Art Smith perform loops, spins, dives, and spirals with his Curtiss Pusher. Right then and there Wiley decided that the life of a pilot was definitely for him.

But in reality, it was back to the farm, and it would be three more years before he was able to leave. Even then, his freedom was short-lived, for he was soon out of money and forced to return home once again. His father promised him the returns for working a ten-acre cotton field, so Wiley resigned himself to the fact that he had no other choice. But after the harvest, he took the crop money and made his escape by enrolling in a seven-month course at the Sweeney Automotive School in Kansas City to learn more about engines. After that he worked for awhile, and then enlisted in the Army Radio School when the war broke out. After the Armistice he refused to return to the farm, electing, instead, the life of a roughneck in the Oklahoma oilfields, but he never lost his desire for flying. His chance finally came in 1924 when the Texas Topknotch Fliers came to town. The group's regular parachute jumper had been injured, so Wiley offered to substitute for him. His first jump was such a thrill that he signed up with the show, but it wasn't long before he could see there was more money to be made in freelancing at up to $200 a jump, so he took off on his own to make ninety-nine jumps in the next two years. By then he had gained enough flight experience to solo, but he still didn't have the money for a plane, so he decided to return to the lucrative oilfields.

That fall, while directing work on a drilling rig, an iron flake, chipped from a bolt, lodged in Wiley's left eye. Infection set in and nothing could be done except to have the eye removed. Wiley wouldn't let that get him down, and during his recuperation he trained his right eye to do the job of two. Then he traded his stroke of bad luck for his dream. With the $1,800 he received from worker's compensation, he purchased a damaged Curtiss Canuck airplane, had it restored, and went to barnstorming.

As the winter of 1927 approached, barnstorming became less than profitable, and it wasn't long before he found himself job hunting. By chance he received a call from oil tycoon F.C. Hall who was looking for someone to pilot the company plane. At $200 a month, Wiley could hardly turn down his offer, but now he could no longer evade getting a commercial license. Federal regulations required good eyesight, and with only one eye, Wiley's only hope was to get a waiver as a trained and experienced pilot. After passing a written test and flying a probationary period of 700 hours he finally received his transportation license on September 16, 1928.

F.C. Hall got tired of open cockpit flying, so when Lockheed Aircraft brought out a streamlined closed cockpit model they called the *Vega*, he needed little selling to purchase one. Naming it the *Winnie Mae* after his daughter, it became the official company plane until the stock market crash, at which time both the plane and pilot were lost to hard times. A couple of years passed before the oil business picked up, and Wiley was back in the air with the *Winnie Mae*. By then Hall was doing so well that he planned to back Wiley in some record-breaking attempts, and they considered the transcontinental record, but scrapped that plan so they could attempt a more unique undertaking of an around-the-world speed flight. The globe had already been circled by the U.S. Army's World Fliers in 1924, but it took them nearly six months for the trip; and the German *Graf Zeppelin* flew the circuit in 21 days in 1929, but Wiley figured he could shorten the record to ten.

Many figured such a speed attempt too risky, especially in view of the limited technology of the time. Hall's partner, Powell Briscoe, agreed and refused to get involved, fearing Post would be killed. Hall looked for other sources of financial backing but failed to get significant support, so the majority of the expenses came out of his own pocket.

With Hall's backing, Wiley flew the Lockheed Vega to Los Angeles for long-range modifications. While there, he visited Harold Gatty in San Diego, to enlist his navigational services which were vitally important to the success of the flight. Radio-beacon air routes were virtually non-existent, weather information sketchy, and quality of aircraft radio was still poor in the early 1930s. After months of retrofitting the plane and physical conditioning by Wiley, the two took off from California in early May of 1931 and headed the *Winnie Mae* toward New York City. After obtaining clearances for landing in other countries, and waiting a month for favorable weather forecasts, they departed Roosevelt Field on Tuesday, June 23, 1931. In the still dark sky, Gatty noted in his log: "Took off at 4:55 daylight-saving time, set course 63 degrees, visibility poor."

With Gatty providing the bearing, Post pointed the *Winnie Mae* for Newfoundland, their first planned stop. Awaiting them were to be hours of blind flying through the North Atlantic weather barrier, fatiguing stretches over the Continent, bogging down in Russia, where only horses and man-power were available to free them, unknown mountains and weather of Siberia, the fog-shrouded Bering Sea, a nose-over in the soft sands of Alaska's shoreline, a lift-off from the main steet of Edmonton, Canada, before arriving back at Roosevelt Field to be welcomed by a crowd of 10,000 cheering onlookers at 8:47 P.M. on July 1st. Their official time for the 15,474 miles covered was 8 days, 15 hours, and 51 minutes, which was 12 days faster than that of the *Graf Zeppelin* two years before. The following day they were greeted in a triumphant welcome by all of New York as they received the largest ticker-tape deluge in the city's history.

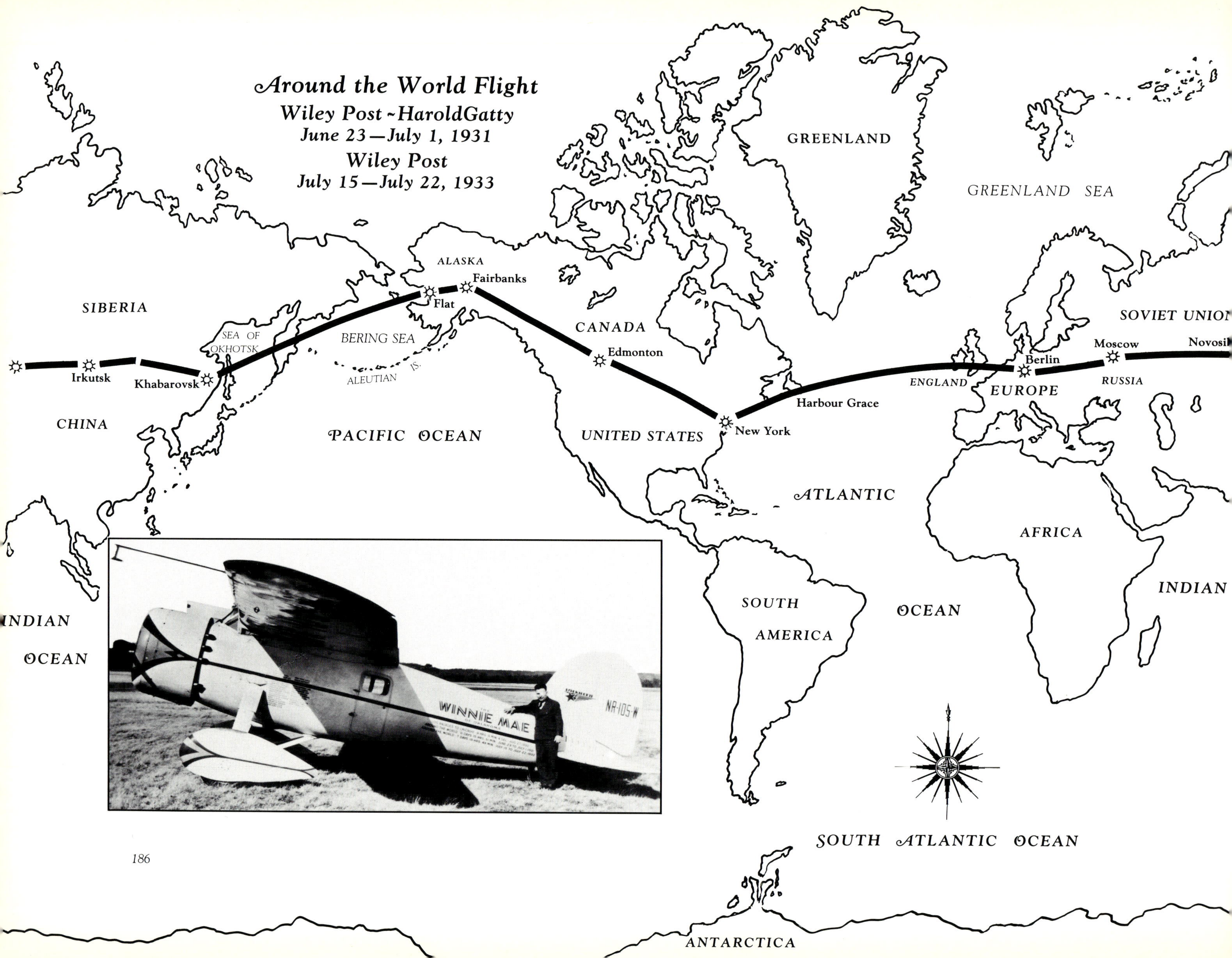
Around the World Flight
Wiley Post ~ HaroldGatty
June 23—July 1, 1931
Wiley Post
July 15—July 22, 1933
GREENLAND
GREENLAND SEA
ALASKA
Fairbanks
Flat
SIBERIA
CANADA
SOVIET UNIO
SEA OF OKHOTSK
BERING SEA
Edmonton
Moscow
Novosi
Berlin
Irkutsk
Khabarovsk
ALEUTIAN IS.
ENGLAND
EUROPE
RUSSIA
Harbour Grace
CHINA
PACIFIC OCEAN
UNITED STATES
New York
ATLANTIC
AFRICA
INDIAN
INDIAN
OCEAN
SOUTH AMERICA
OCEAN
WINNIE MAE
NR-105-W
SOUTH ATLANTIC OCEAN
ANTARCTICA

To the nation, they were heroes, but Post labeled the flight just a stunt without any special significance for aviation, though it did prove his point that whatever an airship could do, the airplane could do better. Even though he was pleased with their achievement, he was not altogether content and started setting his sights on trying it again, but this time solo.

The *Winnie Mae* was rapidly becoming obsolete. New, all-metal, twin-engined aircraft were in the process of development, but a new airplane was far beyond Post's slim finances. In addition to a bit of new equipment, he could only afford a modified engine and an increased fuel capacity of 645 gallons.

In the spring of 1933 a much improved *Winnie Mae* rolled out of the shops, and by early summer, Wiley was ready to try the world trip again. Just like in 1931, reports of bad weather over the North Atlantic kept him grounded for a full month. Finally, after midnight of Saturday, July 15, a favorable forecast came to hand and he decided to go.

After so many false starts in the preceeding weeks, it was remarkable that almost 500 persons had maintained a vigil at New York's Floyd Bennett Airfield throughout the night in hopes of witnessing Post's takeoff.

Arriving at the field, dressed in his atypical flyer's uniform of a snappy dark gray double-breasted suit, white shirt with a blue tie, and a white patch over his left eye, Wiley kissed his wife, Mae, goodbye, climbed up on the *Winnie Mae*, and dropped through the latch in her cockpit. With a last-minute check of instruments, he opened the throttle, released the brakes, and at 5:10 A.M., on July 15th, the *Winnie Mae* roared down the runway. Her tail came up, and after a 1,900 foot run, she was airborne, leaving behind the crowd of well-wishers and curiosity-seekers standing quietly on the tarmac, watching the small, white airplane climb over the bay, and gradually fade into the new light of dawn. Not more than five minutes out, Wiley was into a wall of fog. Turning on his Sperry Autopilot, he headed for the rocky coast of Nova Scotia.

A few hours out, the sky began clearing. Soon he was able to tune in a broadcasting station at St. Johns, Newfoundland, enabling him to navigate with his radio compass. The clear skies continued halfway across the Atlantic until he ran into the weather front that had kept him grounded the past few days. Ahead was fog and rain-filled clouds, so Post climbed to 11,000 feet but found nothing but more clouds and rain. Flying through the thick of the storm, he finally picked up a welcomed signal from the British radio, something new since he and Gatty had flown the same route just two years before. Nearing the British Isles, the weather began to break and he was able to drop below the cloud base to fly across the Irish Sea. Hugging a low altitude, he began having problems with the autopilot which was to plague him the rest of the trip.

Twenty-five hours and 45 minutes from takeoff, Post and his *Winnie Mae* touched down in Berlin, completing the first nonstop airplane flight from New York to the German city. Losing precious time during fueling and attempts to repair his navigational system, he took off for East Prussia, and then discovered further difficulties when a bad leak developed in the oil supply line to the servo unit. Flying on, he ran into bad weather, so landed at Koenigsberg to seek help, but to no avail. Laying over for some much needed rest, he took off the next morning, detouring to Moscow to seek assistance. After two hours, the Russian mechanics were not able to get the Sperry Autopilot in perfect order, so Wiley decided against any more delays, taking off for a stressful flight to Novosibirsk, Siberia. Over half the distance had to be flown blind, and after nearly scraping a hillside that was partially concealed in the fog, he climbed to 21,000 feet to get above the bad weather, but failed to reach the top. The worst part of the trip was having to work his way through a pass in the Ural Mountains at a point where the peaks were 6,000 feet higher than the altitude he was flying. Visibility was so poor that he had to land twice enroute before reaching Novosibirsk, where he stopped only long enough to refuel.

He was in such a rush to get on his way that he didn't even take time out for a bite of food, but that was consistent with his habitual practice of always eating lightly on such long flights.

Continuing eastward, he carried with him a hand-lettered page of instructions prepared by the Russians to accompany maps they collected for his remaining flight over Russia. Once again the autopilot forced another unscheduled landing, this time at Irkutsk. There were reports of storms to the east over the Baikal Mountains, so Post stayed several hours while the Russian mechanics worked on his equipment.

As he continued on, he ran into more visibility problems during the evening darkness before stopping at Rukhlovo and Khabarovsk, where he refueled. Ahead, he faced a 3,100-mile flight to Fairbanks, a trek almost as long as his first-day flight from New York to Berlin, but by this stage of his journey he was by no means as fresh. Along the route stretched the Sea of Okhotsk, the Kamchatka Peninsula with mountains up to 15,000 feet, and then the long stretch of the Bering Sea.

By now Post teetered on the edge of exhaustion, and the weather was not cooperating. For the next seven hours, he flew by instruments and autopilot. When he finally flew out of the murk he found himself flying at 14,000 feet above a great cloud layer over the Gulf of Anadyr. Within a few hours he could see the mountains of Alaska's Seward Peninsula. He began letting down to follow the coastline southeast to Nome. Contacting the local radio station, he sped off into the east for Fairbanks and the Yukon.

Now his radio began giving him trouble, and he couldn't pick up Fairbanks. Being unfamiliar with the terrain, afflicted by poor visibility, and worn by fatigue, Post was wandering around Alaska's skies, looking for a landmark that he could correspond to something on his charts that would provide a bearing for a course to the Alaskan city. Finally he saw the small mining town of Flat below him, 300 miles southwest of Fairbanks.

The airfield at Flat was nothing more than a crude landing strip. The *Winnie Mae* came down lightly and rolled to the end of the strip, but Wiley was unable to brake in time to avoid a ditch. The plane lurched over on her right wing, crumbling the right leg of her landing gear. Her tail came up, driving her nose into the earth, bending the propeller. Luckily, the weary Post was not injured, and the plane was not badly damaged, but it couldn't fly. An emergency radio signal was sent out to Fairbanks for Alaska bush pilot Joe Crosson, and he promptly took off for Flat with his mechanic and a servicable fixed-pitch propeller.

Post got some much needed rest, but was up at dawn to find the plane repaired and ready to go. He followed Crosson to Fairbanks where the weather forced an eight-hour delay. Even after takeoff, he faced more bad weather, and it was mostly blind flying to Edmonton, Canada where he refueled. From there it was a clear, 2,000-mile run home.

Great excitement was mounting in New York City as news of his flight began filling the radio airwaves, and Extras flooded the city's newstands in anticipation of Post's return. All of the roads leading to Bennett Field were hopelessly jammed with traffic, and a crowd estimated at 50,000 people crowded around waiting for him. Out of the darkness came the sound of the *Winnie Mae*'s Wasp engine, then came the glow of the landing lights floating through the night sky, across the field boundary, and onto the runway.

At the instant of touchdown at 11:50 P.M. on July 22, 1933, Wiley Post and his *Winnie Mae* had completed their second trip around the world. As he taxied up to the terminal building, the plane was engulfed in a swarm of humanity. As he lifted himself through the overhead hatch in the cockpit, Wiley greeted his wife and the same friends who had seen him off just 7 days, 18 hours, and 49½ minutes before. What is most unique is that he was the first person to circumnavigate the earth twice by aircraft, and the first to fly it solo, a record that has never been duplicated under similar circumstances.

Solo Flight

Nancy Kistler was exceptionally fortunate in learning to fly, as she had an advantage over most other would-be pilots—she happened to be very friendly with an employee of Tex Rankin's Flying Service in Portland, Oregon. With some special lessons and flying tips, she was ready to solo after just seven hours in Tex's old *Jenny* biplane. For a girl of sixteen it was a real thrill to be able to take off alone on the Swan Island airstrip and head up the Columbia River all by herself. It was a beautiful day for flying, and she didn't have a care in the world, that is until the engine sputtered and died. Luckily, there happened to be some open pasture along the river bottom and she was able to execute a dead-stick landing in a field near Troutdale. She didn't have any trouble getting the plane down safely, but when it rolled into a field of crops she was suddenly scared to death. She looked back over the tracks the plane had left and wondered how in the world she would ever get out of such a mess. About then the farmer came out to meet her, and she didn't know what to say. This was Depression times, and she didn't have money to pay for any crop damage, nor to have the plane worked on so she could get back to the airfield.

Fortunately, the farmer wasn't mad. Checking over the airplane, he discovered only that it was out of gas. Nancy was all apologetic and remarked, "I'm so sorry. I have no money to pay for the damage or for any gasoline."

The farmer told her not to worry and invited her to join him and his wife for lunch.

The couple were so nice, Nancy wondered what she could do to make things right. The farmer thought for a moment, and then said, "How about getting a ride in that flying machine so I can have a look from up in the air, and wave to my neighbors?"

Of course, for a girl of sixteen, on her first solo flight, she had no right to haul a passenger, but she didn't know what else to do. So after filling the tank with gas, the farmer climbed aboard, Nancy taxied the *Jenny* to open pasture, and took off to fly from one farm to the next so the farmer could have his aerial adventure and impress all of his neighbors.

Nancy's next trip out was to be a cross-country solo flight from Swan Island. She planned to fly over the interstate bridge that spanned the Columbia, and land at Pearson Field on the Washington side of the river. Everything was fine until she couldn't get the altitude to make it over the bridge, so she decided to go under it like she had seen so many other pilots do—only she didn't realize no sane pilot would attempt such a feat at this time of year, for the Columbia River was at the flood stage and there was very little space between the water and the bridge structure. The pilots and ground crew at Pearson were horrified when they saw what she was attempting, but there was nothing they could do but stare in disbelief. Happy as a lark, Nancy started her path and against all odds, with only inches to spare on all sides, made it through, even flying blind, for the spinning prop pulled water from the river's surface and dumped it all back into the cockpit. Not being able to see, she held her course and pulled back on the stick to clear the water, and then landed at the airfield looking like a drowned rat.

The outcome of the next three flights were about the same as her first one—never any trouble in taking off, but not too far out the plane's motor would sputter and die. Being young and naive to the ways of the world, she didn't realize that some of the other pilots were routinely draining her gas tank so they could fly a little longer. Luckily, she was able to find a clear landing space in each instance, and her experiences made her much wiser; she began checking her gas tank before each flight. She also became somewhat of a celebrity, gaining the unofficial title of the *Forced Landing Queen of the Northwest*.

The Ill-Fated Gee Bees

It is apparent that Zantford Granville, 'Granny' for short, was born with an inventive nature. By 1922 he was running a garage in Arlington, Massachusetts, but that didn't seem to satisfy him, as he had a growing fascination with flying. And that was a problem: he was petrified of heights. Just climbing to the top of the barn scared the daylights out of him, leaving him numb with fear for days afterward. But he finally screwed up courage enough to take a ride in an old Curtiss *Jenny*, and discovered that his fear of heights did not translate into a fear of flying.

Not long after that he drew out his severance pay to go in business for himself, leaving his brother to tend the shop. He bought an old car, added a truck body and placed a sign proclaiming "Granny's Mobile Aeroplane-fixing service". Since many of the airplanes of the 1920's were not the best of design and construction, he didn't lack for business.

Although he was busy, his inventive nature kept nagging him so it wasn't long before he conjured up the idea of designing and building his own plane. His four brothers liked the sound of that and it soon became a brotherly spare-time, evening, weekend, and holiday project.

From their efforts was born the Gee Bee Model-One, shortened to *G.B.* for the Granville Brothers. Impatience to test fly their baby got the best of Granny, and he ended up taking the maiden flight during a thunderstorm in the middle of the night. The bad weather and darkness were bad enough, but he didn't even have a parachute, as he couldn't wait long enough for one to arrive. His reason for the night flight, he said, was that he didn't want anyone laughing at him in case anything went wrong. Luckily, nothing did, and the brothers were now in the airplane building business.

They turned out eight more of their Model A biplanes before the Great Depression when nearly everyone quit buying private planes.

Hanging on to their dream, the boys hired a designer, figuring that a more modern version would be in demand. The result was their Gee Bee Sportster, a little low-wing monoplane fitted with a 110-hp Cirrus engine. With it they entered the 1930 All-American Flying Derby and finished second, giving them encouragement to press on. New models were designed, but they still weren't making any money, so Granny had the idea to build a racer to enter in the 1931 National Air Races where there was some money to be won.

Starting in mid-July, they had their pickle-barrel shaped Model Z racer equipped with a racing Wasp engine and ready to fly by late August. At the Nationals, Lowell Bayles, who'd flown their Sportster in the Aerial Derby, won the Goodyear race at 206 mph, the Thompson at 236 mph, and the Shell Speed Dash at 267 mph.

It was miraculous! These five farm boys, with only grade school educations, had produced just about the fastest plane in the world, and in a mere six weeks. It was an incredible record...if only they had stopped there.

But they weren't really satisfied; they had their eyes on the world speed record, too. Obtaining an even bigger Wasp engine from Pratt & Whitney—a 750-hp monster—they installed it in their Model Z. From then on everything went downhill.

In Detroit, Lowell Bayles was again piloting, and his record attempts were going badly; then on his last try a fuel cap came loose, smashing the windshield and clouting him in the eye. In his attempt to recover, the Model Z pitched up, one wing folded back, and the Gee Bee rolled over and over. Bayles was killed instantly as the plane hit the ground and burst into a ball of flame.

More Super Sportsters were built, crashed, rebuilt, and crashed again. Even their major backer, Russel Boardman, spun in while testing one, putting himself in the hospital.

Things picked up in the fall of 1932 when the great Jimmy Doolittle agreed to pilot the Granville R-1 racer at the Nationals in Cleveland, Ohio. Like previous models, the new Gee Bee retained the distinctive stubby design and other bad characteristics: forward visibility for take-off and landing was clearly nil, and the elevator and rudder handling were a battle against the torque of a 800-hp engine mounted to a fuselage less than 18 feet in length.

As soon as Doolittle got to Cleveland he took the R-1 up to practice pylon turns. Fortunately, he climbed to 5,000 feet before trying any maneuvers, for without warning, the plane did two snap rolls before he could bring it under control. If he had been at the normal racing altitude of 250 or lower, he would have become another G. B. statistic.

The R-1 was surely a strange plane to fly, but when Doolittle took off in the meet, it went like a bullet all the way to a new world landplane speed record of 296 mph; two days later he captured the Thompson Trophy at 253 mph. His performance with the Gee Bee was a rare feat of airmanship, but once was enough. Within a few weeks, Doolittle retired from racing altogether, convinced that the cost of air racing in lives and equipment had grown far too high.

After the two wins at Cleveland, it was back downhill for the Granvilles. In 1933 the transcontinental race was east to west for the Nationals in Los Angeles. Coming in to refuel at Indianapolis, Russell Thaw, piloting the R-2, lost it on touchdown, hit a wingtip and ground-looped. Right behind him was Russell Boardman in the R-1, now powered by a colossal 900-hp Hornet. After gassing up he took off; and no sooner was he in the air than a wind change caught the plane, stalling it, which caused it to roll and slide down the field upside down. Suffering a cracked skull, Boardman never regained consciousness.

11

BENDIX
EVENT L LAP
TIME

The brothers patched up the R-2, but when pilot Jimmy Haizlip attempted a landing, he touched down a bit crooked. The wing dropped and the plane snap-rolled, then dug in a wingtip and went cartwheeling end over end down the field. Though bruised and battered, Haizlip wasn't hurt too seriously, but virtually nothing was left of the R-2.

Before the year was out, Florence Klingensmith lost control of her Senior Sportster in the Chicago races when fabric tore from one wing. She jumped, but was too low for the chute to open. Her death was followed early the next year by Granny himself when he spun in while delivering one of his Sportsters in bad weather.

Granville Brothers Aircraft was sold soon afterward, and that should have been the end of the Gee Bees, but somehow the brothers found the money to finish a new and bigger racer they had been working on before Granny's death. This new model, they called the "Q.E.D.", was a stretch Gee Bee designed for long-range flying. Unlike its counterparts, it flew on for a number of years without any mishaps. Then it was bought by ace Mexican flyer Francisco Sarabia, who renamed it the *Conquistador del Cielo*. On May 24, 1939, he set a speed record by flying nonstop from Mexico City to New York City in 10 hours 47 minutes. A few days later, taking off from Bolling Field in Washington, D.C. on his homeward journey, a rag carelessly left inside the cowling was sucked into the carburetor. The plane faltered and fell into the Potomac River, making Sarabia the fifth and last victim of the ill-fated Gee Bees.

Roscoe and Gilmore

Roscoe Turner, sporting a waxed mustache, and dressed in a powder blue military-style uniform that he designed himself, was without question the most flamboyant pilot who ever graced the airways.

Having his first taste of flying in 1917, Turner decided to stick with it. He made a name for himself in the deep South by standing on the top wing of a biplane while dropping leaflets over cities to announce the premier of the Hollywood movie ***Soldiers of Fortune***. Then his first recognition as a racer came in 1929 with a sensational transcontinental flight, carrying passengers from New York to Los Angeles in 20 hours and 20 minutes, and then returning in 18 hours and 30 minutes.

Purely and simply, he was a speed merchant. Calling himself Colonel Roscoe Turner, he dominated the race circuit, setting new transcontinental speed records in 1932, 1933, and again in 1934. Then he teamed up with Clyde Pangborn to race in the 1934 London-to-Melbourne McRobertson International Air Derby. Flying a Boeing 247-D, America's first twin-engined, low-winged, all-metal passenger transport, they made the 11,300-mile trip in 92 hours, 55 minutes, and 30 seconds to place second in the speed division.

Flying his Wedell-Williams racer that same year, he won the Thompson Trophy race, then won it again in 1938 and 1939 with his Laird-Turner LRT-14 Meteor, and probably would have won it a fourth time if he hadn't thought that he shaved a pylon too close and went back to circle it again. He also won the Bendix race in 1933 and again in 1944.

Although he won more prize money in racing than any other pilot on the circuit, he constantly teetered between lavish solvency and bankruptcy. He loved speed, and his addiction to flying and aviation was so great that he spent more than twice his total prize winnings to develop faster, more reliable aircraft, planes which could outspeed by far the fastest fighters in the military.

Although Turner's racing abilities brought him wide renown, he was probably best remembered for his traveling companion while flying for the Gilmore Oil Company.

It was in 1930 that a most garish inspiration occurred to Turner when he saw the image of a lion on a billboard advertising Gilmore Oil. Lusting at the time for a new plane, he approached Earl Gilmore, the president of the company, with a proposal. If Gilmore would buy a new Lockheed *Air Express* and hire Turner as pilot, he would, in turn, set more speed records and gain "a million dollars worth of publicity" for the company by strapping a live lion—to be named *Gilmore*—into the copilot's seat on every flight.

Earl Gilmore couldn't resist the offer, and promptly wrote a $15,000 check for the *Air Express* which was to sport the Gilmore trademark. Turner wasted no time in ordering the plane and then searched the Yellow Pages under the heading of ***'Lions'***. To his dismay, a full-grown lion cost $200; that's when he put his hustling abilities to work and got the owner to donate a five-week-old lion cub to the cause of advancing aviation. Turner was enthralled with his new pet, and from that day forth they were inseparable.

Gilmore the lion started flying when he was four months old, but by the time he reached six months he had grown too large for the cockpit, so Roscoe had a special seat made so his pal could ride in the cabin compartment. Gilmore even sported his own flying suit, as well as a parachute which the Humane Society required Turner to provide. Fortunately, he never had to test it.

Gilmore's attitude did not always endear himself well with others at the United Airport in Burbank, California, for as he grew up he decided that he was king of the hangar. He was always petrifying unsuspecting visitors by licking the back of their necks with his raspy tongue, and he had a nasty habit of chasing some of the pilots up the hangar wall. Turner always excused his pal's actions, saying that he was just playing with them.

Whenever the two were on the road they were a promotor's dream. The $15,000 that Earl Gilmore spent for the agreement with Turner was the best advertising investment that he could have made. Photographers across the nation clamored to get pictures of Roscoe and Gilmore together. Even the best hotels offered them luxury suites, registering them as *Roscoe & Gilmore*. This continued until Gilmore was eventually grounded after 25,000 flying miles. He had at last grown too large to continue the aerial excursions.

From then on, his remaining days were spent at a small zoo in Los Angeles, never forgotten by Turner who sent a monthly $40 check to buy meat for his buddy. Then, when Gilmore died at the age of seventeen, Turner had him stuffed and placed in his trophy room, assuring his guests, "He's not one one of the trophies, they belong to him as much as they do to me."

Gilmore remained there to share in the glory of the racing years until Turner's death, at which time his estate was directed to resettle Gilmore in Washington's Smithsonian Air Museum so he could continue his reign in aviation history.

Chapter

7

Last Flight

Prediction Come True

Wiley Post just wasn't content unless he was flying or planning some kind of aerial excursion into the unknown. After his two around-the-world trips and flights into the stratosphere, it was rumored that Pan American Airways was backing him for a feasibility study of an airmail and passenger route between Alaska and Russia, but then they backed out. Post had his heart set on a trip, and thought that it would be nice to have some company for a change. This brought to mind humorist Will Rogers, as the two had a mutual interest in aviation. Rogers loved to fly, and they had been friends since meeting after Wiley's 1931 world flight.

Rogers was indeed interested. He was exhausted from his last movie, ***Steamboat Round the Bend***, and he also felt that the quality of his syndicated newspaper column was deteriorating. Believing that a trip to Alaska and possibly on to Russia would give him new material for his column, he was thrilled to have the chance to go.

Post had retired his trusty *Winnie Mae*, and had since acquired a low-wing hybrid made up from parts of two previously damaged aircraft. The wings of a Lockheed Explorer had been added to the body of a Lockheed Orion, thereby creating his *Orion Explorer*. Because of expected water landings, he needed pontoons for the trip and arranged the loan of a set from Alaska bush pilot, Joe Crosson. The pontoons were to be installed in Seattle, but when Post and Rogers got there, the requested floats had not yet arrived. Rogers was impatient to be on the way, and since he was paying the expenses, Post looked for a backup set of pontoons.

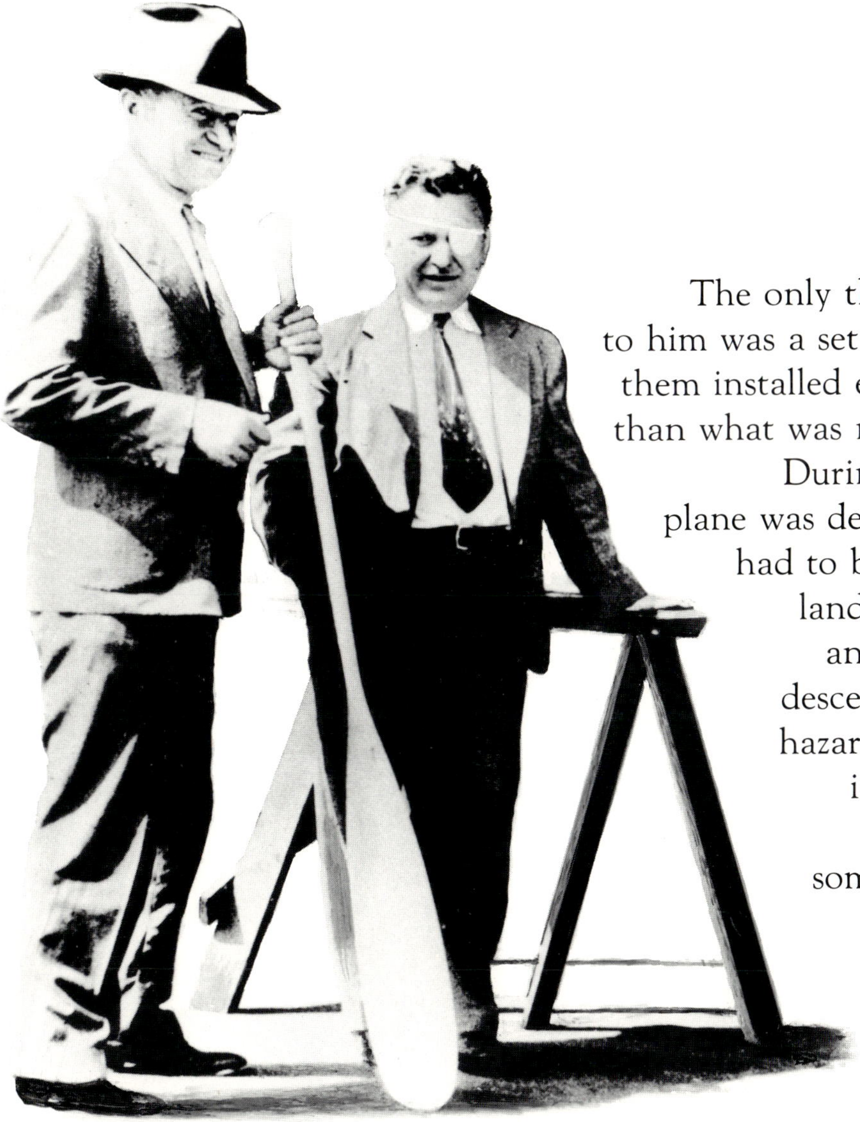

The only thing he could find readily available to him was a set from a Fokker trimotor, so he had them installed even though they were much larger than what was needed on his hybrid Orion.

During a test run he discovered that his plane was decidedly nose-heavy and that power had to be carried to keep the nose up for a landing. Without power, the nosedown angle became so steep and the rate of descent so fast, that a water landing was hazardous. However, with Rogers settled in the aft section of the aircraft, the nose-heaviness could be overcome somewhat. The plane could have been modified to solve the problem, but Wiley worried about the delay for government approval, so the two lost no time in departing from Seattle's Lake Washington.

Will and Wiley

Landing at Juneau to visit friends, their stay was prolonged several days because of rain. After the weather cleared, they flew to Dawson in Yukon Territory, and then on to Fairbanks, Alaska. Upon their arrival they visited with Joe Crosson. During the visit, Rogers developed an interest in Charlie Brower, an old-time trader and whaler who lived at Point Barrow for nearly half a century, and was often referred to as King of the Artic. Rogers thought an interview with him would be ideal for a newspaper story.

Post agreed to fly to Point Barrow, but Crosson advised against it until they made some changes to the *Orion-Explorer*. He was disturbed by the nose-heaviness of the plane, and predicted that a crash would result if its engine quit at low altitude, especially during takeoff or landing.

This made sense to Post, but Rogers, having complete confidence in his companion's flying, was anxious to get under way. There was no question about Post's ability as a pilot, but he had very little experience with seaplanes. Being fully aware of this, he took every precaution accordingly, except that Rogers had fronted the money and was anxious to get underway. Wiley decided to take the risk.

From Fairbanks, Post radioed the government weather station in Barrow for a report on conditions and was told that snow, sleet, and zero visibility made a landing impossible; but after waiting a day Wiley decided they could make it.

Seeing that their minds were made up, Crosson advised Wiley to head for Anaktuvuk Pass of the Brooks Range and fly directly north until he sighted the Artic Ocean, then head due west, hugging the coast until he reached Point Barrow, a V-shaped peninsula that jutted into the Polar Sea.

Just before noon on August 15th, Post and Rogers were ready for takeoff from the Chena River which is narrow and winding. Because of the hazard, Wiley only partially filled the plane's tanks so he wouldn't have to attempt lifting off under a full load. There was no problem getting airborne and Wiley turned the plane north to Lake Harding where arrangements had been made to stockpile additional fuel for their trip.

Landing at the lake, Post topped off the tanks and took to the air for the next leg of their journey. Passing over the village of Wiseman, he headed the plane through a notch in the mountain barrier, and right into the face of an Artic storm front.

Reports of hearing his plane from the ground indicated that Post was flying blind and had become lost somewhere along the route, for he had skirted the coastline for awhile and then turned due west. Finally getting a break in the clouds, he sighted some water and set the plane down on a small lagoon named Walakpa. As luck would have it, there was an Eskimo camp on the shore where some men were fishing. Wiley taxied over, cut the engine, and he and Will climbed out to talk with Clair Okpeaha and his wife who taught in the Barrow Sunday School and knew English fairly well. After Wiley asked directions to Point Barrow, Will spent a little time inquiring about the Eskimo activities, and then the two climbed back aboard the plane, waved, and taxied to one end of the lagoon to start their takeoff. Since the lagoon was too small for Post to make a preliminary run to warm up the engine, his first pass had to be the only one.

Post pushed open the throttle, revving the engine to a deafening pitch as they headed for take off. Twin sprays of water frothed from the floats as the plane came up on the steps, lifted off, banked to the right, and headed toward Barrow. Suddenly the engine quit. True to Joe Crosson's prediction, without power, the *Explorer* dove straight into the water, throwing gravel and spray in all directions. The impact was horrific.

The plane came to rest on her back, with a broken fuselage and fractured wing. A small fire blazed, but immediately self-extinguished. Then there was silence except for the lapping of waves against the wreckage.

The Eskimoes were terrified. Okpeaha was in a state of shock, but ventured close enough to call out, hoping for a response. Time after time he called, but there was no answer. Leaving the others behind to stare in disbelief at the broken hull in the water, he started running toward Barrow for help.

It took five hours for him to cover the sixteen miles through tundra grass, skirting dozens of lakes and bogs, before staggering into the store in Barrow. Almost too exhausted to speak, he described the crash to the store owner, who called the local school teacher, Frank Dougherty. He in turn phoned Sergeant Stanley Morgan, the Signal Corps man in charge of the Point Barrow weather station. At that point it occurred to no one that it was Post and Rogers who had crashed. Since they had been warned of the weather, and were not expected for several days, no one even considered it could be them.

Dougherty, Morgan, and a group of Eskimoes headed out in a launch. Charlie Brower outfitted a faster one and dispatched his son David in charge. The rescue party was well on its way before Okpeaha recovered his composure enough to describe the occupants of the plane. It was not until he mentioned, "Other man short, have sore eye, rag over eye." that it suddenly dawned on Morgan who must have been in the plane.

It was three o'clock in the morning when Charlie Brower and Dr. Greist heard the launches returning. From the sounds they knew the worst had happened, for the motors of the launches were throttled down to normal speed, and the Eskimoes were chanting their plaintive death song.

Sergeant Morgan lost no time in sending word of the tragedy to the outside world, but it took two relays and nearly two hours to reach the continental United States. From there the news flashed around the nation.

When the story appeared in newspapers it overshadowed everything else that was going on in the world. Four full pages of the ***New York Times*** were devoted to the event on Saturday, August 17; Sunday's edition was nearly the same, and for a week the newspaper and radio coverage continued.

Perhaps not since the death of Abraham Lincoln had a tragedy touched so many Americans as did the loss of Will Rogers and Wiley Post. Oklahoma may have lost two of her native sons, but the entire nation was poorer for it.

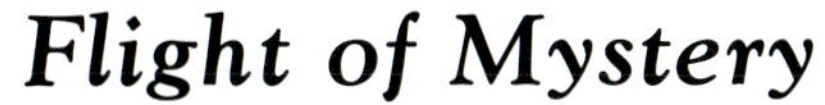

Flight of Mystery

With the chocks pulled from beneath her wheels, the Lockheed Electra moved down the runway, and thirty seconds later she was airborne. Amelia Earhart and her navigator, Fred Noonan, were on their way around the world.

Leveling off over the Florida Straights, Amelia had a chance to reflect back on her life and times. She hadn't always been interested in flying, and it wasn't until her father arranged a flight for her during a California airshow that she became captivated with the thought of becoming a pilot. Seeking out Neta Snook, the first woman graduate of the Curtiss School of Aviation, Amelia began lessons on the installment plan. If she had money, she flew, if not, she worked. Under such circumstances it was 1921 before she soloed, only to discover that there were no jobs for women pilots and that flying for sport was expensive. She resigned herself to staying occupied in social work, but continued flying whenever she had a chance.

A unique opportunity presented itself in 1928 when Mrs. Frederick Guest, a wealthy New York society sportswoman and a group of friends purchased a trimotor Fokker for the purpose of making a flight across the Atlantic. Her family would not consent to her plan to make the trip, but she insisted that a woman should be aboard for the flight. Others in the group were agreeable, and one of them, George Putnam, suggested they contact a flyer who had set a women's record in 1924. An invitation by long-distance telephone was made and accepted without hesitation.

On June 17, 1928, Amelia Earhart became the first woman to cross the Atlantic by air, becoming internationally famous overnight. The press concentrated on Amelia to the extent that the excellent job that Wilmer Stultz and Louis Gordon did in navigating through fog for almost the entire trip was all but ignored. This was embarrassing to her, for she was merely a passenger. All the unearned publicity made her more determined than ever to prove herself as a flier, and in 1929 she had her day when she flew a Lockheed Vega to third place in the Woman's Air Derby. This was followed by experimentation and record-setting with autogiros.

Public admiration continued to grow and she found herself much in demand on the lecture circuit, speaking on the safety of flying and women's place in the air. Then it was on May 18, 1932 that she set off on a flight that brought her international fame. Working her Lockheed Vega up the eastern seaboard, she refueled at Habor Grace, Newfoundland on the evening of May 20th to begin a transatlantic flight to Paris. Flying through storms and plagued by wind, fog, ice buildup, a broken altimeter and tachometer, a leaky gauge on the reserve gas tank, pounding in the exhaust manifold, and spitting flames, she was able to keep the plane in the air until she reached Ireland. Even though she didn't reach her planned destination, she did succeed in crossing the Atlantic, making her the first woman to fly the ocean, the second person to fly it solo; and her flying time of 14 hours and 56 minutes was faster than any previous crossing. News flashed around the world. Following Charles Lindbergh's path of 1927, the *Lady Lindy* had at last proven that women could fly long distances just as well as their male counterparts.

Now, heading around the world, she was pushing the limits again; she assumed this would be her last long journey, for there was nothing left to challenge her.

Flying over the Caribbean, she and Noonan were heading for San Juan, Puerto Rico, the first stop on their global journey. In the succeeding days, their flight down the east coast of South America was uneventful. After a brief rest at Natal, Brazil, the pair left for a tiring 1,900-mile trip over the South Atlantic. Disregarding Noonan's course correcting, Amelia missed their African destination by 160 miles. Passing over 4,400 miles of African wasteland, they pressed on to Assab, then to Karachi, Pakistan. Dodging and fighting the monsoons, they battled their way to Ragoon, Bangkok, and Singapore. Flying out of Bandung, Noonan found a malfunction in their long-range navigational system. Reluctantly they turned back for repairs.

Two days later they were back in the air, heading for Port Darwin to drop off their parachutes to make more space since they would be of no more use while flying over the water. Then they went on to New Guinea, the departure point for the most grueling leg of the flight—2,556 miles to Howland Island, which was just a speck of land in the ocean.

After forty days of flying and 22,000 miles, both pilot and navigator were physically worn out, but still in good spirits.

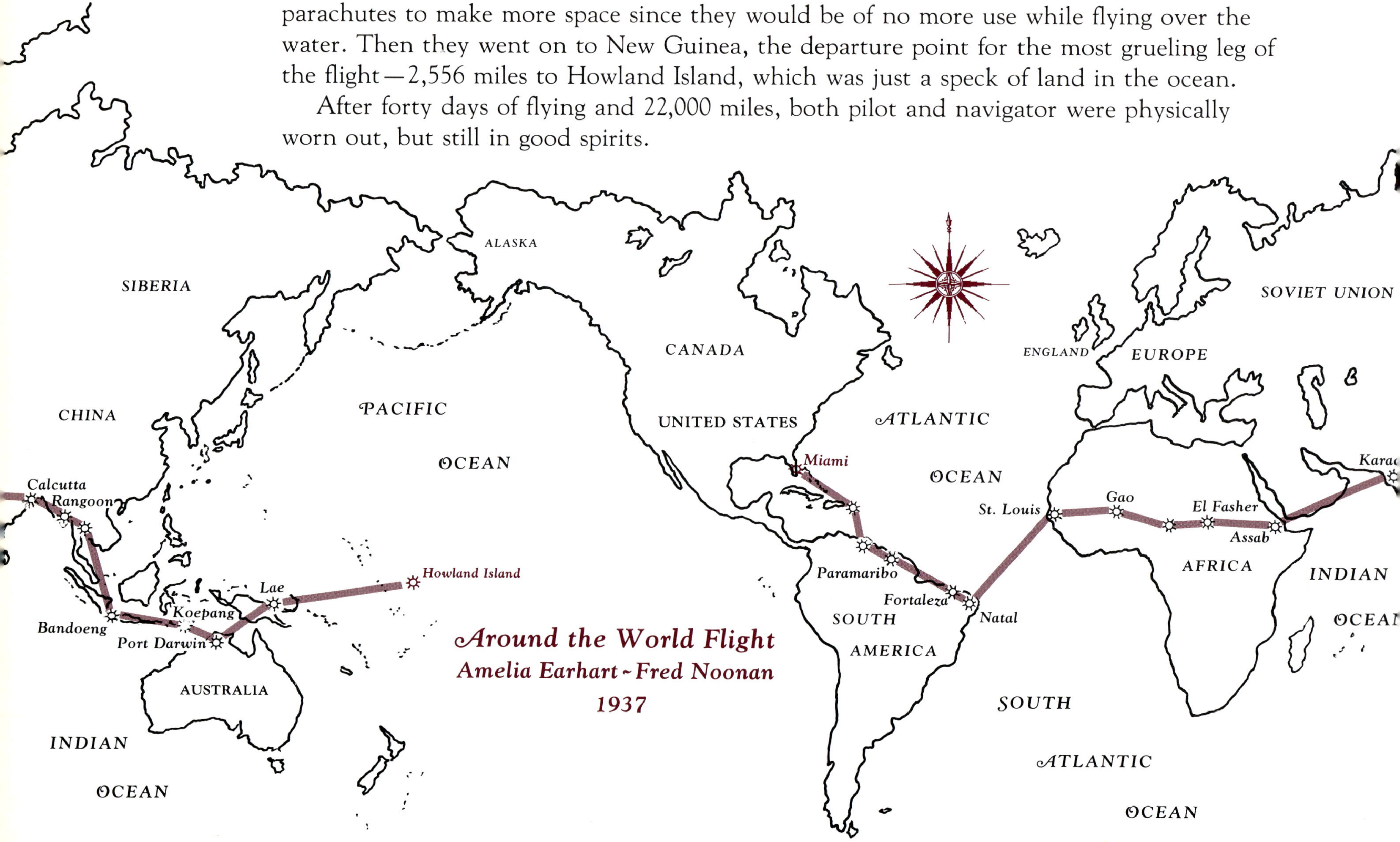

Around the World Flight
Amelia Earhart - Fred Noonan
1937

Taking off, they had no landmarks ahead of them, only celestial navigation and their radio homing station to guide them to Howland, but the radio was useless until they were within close range. There was a 250-foot reel-type trailing antenna that was supposed to be with the plane, but Amelia had that removed in Miami to avoid the trouble of reeling it in and out. Now, 800 miles out of New Guinea, she and Noonan realized that she had made a mistake of leaving it, but everything was going well, so there was no cause for alarm. Besides, the Coast Guard cutter *Itasca* was waiting off Howland Island to pick up their signals.

Aboard the cutter that night, everything had been checked in preparation for the Electra to come within range. Shortly after midnight, the radioman made the first attempt to contact the world flyers, first by voice, then by key with their homing signal. Transmissions continued, but by 1:15 in the morning they had not raised the pair. Commander Thompson of the *Isasca* wasn't worried as the plane was still an estimated 1,000 miles out.

Then at 2:45 A.M., Howland time, with the plane tentatively fixed at 800 miles, Amelia Earhart's voice was indistinctly heard through heavy stactic, "...cloudy and overcast...", then nothing. Spirits soared aboard the cutter; they had heard her! They were coming in.

That night of July 2, 1937 was hot and sweltering: temperature 81 degrees, humidity high, wind calm, and clear skies over Howland Island. The Electra had been out eleven hours and forty-five minutes, flying through intermittent thunderstorms. According to Leo Bellarts, Chief Radioman on the *Itasca*, she should arrive in about six hours. He called San Francisco and advised them.

Off and on, for the next six hours, the *Itasca* transmitted the weather by key and by voice, and then sent out the homing signal. Occasionally, they made voice contact, but the message was still garbled. Radios on the ship and on Howland Island were unable to get a bearing.

Then at 6:45 A.M., Amelia Earhart's voice, strong and clear, but with an undertone of urgency broke through, "Please take a bearing on us, and report in half an hour. We're about a hundred miles out!" Again, the Howland directional finder was unable to get a bearing. The *Itasca* continued trying to reach her, but to no avail.

At 7:42, Amelia's voice broke through, "We must be on you, but cannot see you... gas is running low...been unable to reach you by radio...flying at 1,000 feet."

The *Itasca* acknowledged, and then repeated, "Your message OK....Please acknowledge." Nine minutes later Amelia called again, and by now it was obvious that she had heard none of the cutter's transmissions.

Then her voice came through again, "KHAQQ to Itasca...We're circling, but cannot hear you...go ahead on 7500 now or schedule time of half hour."

The radioman sent out a long homing signal on 7500 kilocycles. Then momentary success—she called back, "Receiving your signals, but unable to get a minimum. Please take a bearing on us and answer with voice on 3105." She then whistled into the microphone while the *Itasca* and Howland station worked frantically to get a radio fix, but there was too much static. Once again their attempts failed.

At 8:33 the *Itasca* called again and informed the Electra that they were transmitting constantly on 7500 kilocycles. There was no answer; ship's radio operator requested a reply be made on 3105.

At 8:45 A.M., Amelia Earhart's voice broke through in urgency, "We are in a line of position 157-337. We are running north and south." Then there was nothing.

For over an hour the radio operators on the *Itasca* and on Howland Island tried again and again to make contact, but there was only silence.

It seemed that Noonan had taken a shot on the sun, and they were flying on a north-south line looking for the island. At 10:15 Commander Thompson ordered the *Itasca* north, reasoning that if the plane had flown south, it would have spotted Baker Island, thirty-eight miles away. The *337* line, he decided, was the one to search. Hopefully, if the fliers had to ditch, the empty tanks of the Electra would keep them afloat.

Orders from Washington rallied the carrier *Lexington*, with full complement of aircraft, a seaplane, and six other ships into action, touching off the greatest sea hunt in history. The vast search itself proved to be a fiasco—chasing down false leads, the hunt became hopelessly disorganized, causing aimless scurrying over a quarter million square miles of reefs, islands, and empty sea. Aircraft logged 1,600 hours in scanning 150,000 square miles of ocean surface. All the while a stunned America listened to its radios, hoping each minute that a news broadcast would bring word of the rescue of the nation's most famous aviatrix and her navigator companion. But there was nothing. Speculation led to more speculation, but their disappearance remained a mystery. Some believed the two were flying a spy mission for the U.S. Government, and were captured and killed by the Japanese; others believed they simply ran out of gas and vanished into Pacific waters.

For over fifty years, the truth has continued to nag historians, and the search goes on to this day to solve one of aviation's most intriguing mysteries. Whatever the outcome, there is no question that the disappearance of Amelia Earhart and Fred Noonan was a national tragedy, but they are still remembered, and have taken their place in the annals of aviation along with the other women and men who dreamed and dared to venture forth as pioneers of the sky.

End of an aerial excursion for J.R. Doty

Historical Notes

1783 . . . Nov 21—Montgolfier brothers launch their hot air balloon with Pilarre de Rozier and d'Arlandes aboard to make the first flight in history.

1797 . . . Oct 22—from a balloon, Garnerin makes the first parachute jump in history.

1804 . . . Sir George Cayley, first man in the world to identify and correctly record the parameters of heavier-than-air flight, uses model glider for research.

1852 . . . Cayley's glider is the first heavier-than-air craft to carry a man in flight.

. . . Sept 24—Frenchman Henri Gifford, equipped with a cigar-shaped airship with a propeller and lightweight steam engine, makes a 17-mile flight over Paris.

1880 . . . July 4 - Little Falls, New York—Flying as "*Carlotta, the Lady Aeronaut*", Mary H. Myers is the first woman to make a solo balloon flight.

1889 . . . Octave Chanute first publishes his book ***Progress in Flying Machines***, as a series of magazine articles.

1891 . . . German brothers Otto and Gustave Lilienthal construct first of their fixed-wing monoplane and biplane gliders which fly over 750 feet in distance.

1893 . . . Octave Chanute makes the first successful flight with a triplane glider.

1901 . . . Samuel Langley launches his model airplane fitted with a petrol engine to achieve the world's first successful unmanned powered flight.

1903 . . . Dec 17 - Kitty Hawk, North Carolina—Wright brothers, with Orville at the controls, make the first powered, sustained, and controlled airplane flight in history—their *Flyer* travels 120 feet in a 12-sec duration.

1905 . . . June—first fully practical powered airplane, the *Flyer III* is flown by the Wright brothers.

. . . Oct 5 - Dayton, Ohio—Wright brothers set world distance record of 24 miles at Huffman Prairie.

1907 . . . July—Aeronautical Division of the Signal Corps formed.

1908 . . . May 14—first passenger ever to fly in an aeroplane is Charles Furnas who is taken aloft by Wilbur Wright for a 28-sec duration.

. . . June 20—first American to fly after the Wrights is Glenn Curtiss in his *June Bug* biplane.

. . . Sept 17 - Ft. Myers, Virginia—Lt. T.E. Selfridge becomes the first fatality in powered flight during Orville Wright's U.S. Army acceptance trials.

. . . Dec - Auvours, France—Wilbur Wright sets world altitude record of 360 feet and distance record of 77 miles in 2 hrs and 20 min with his *Flyer* biplane.

. . . Glenn L. Martin builds his first pusher biplane.

1909 . . . July—for $25,000 plus a $5,000 bonus for exceeding a speed of 40 mph, the Wright biplane, *Miss Columbia*, becomes the first aeroplane purchased by the U.S. Government.

. . . Aug 1 - San Francisco—Geneve Shaffer, flying a glider built by her brother Cleve, is the first woman pilot in America.

. . . August - Rheims, France—Glenn Curtiss wins the Bennett Cup with a speed of 47 mph with his *Golden Flyer* powered by a V-8, water-cooled, 50-hp engine.

. . . a Universal News cameraman rides with Wilbur Wright to take the first movies from a plane in flight.

. . . Dec 9 - Mineola, New York—first American monoplane to fly is the *Walden III*, designed by Dr. Henry Walden.

1910 . . . Record flight for the 152-mile distance between Albany and New York City by Glenn Curtiss in 2 hrs, 51 min with an average speed of 52 mph in his Curtiss pusher.

. . . Jan 10-20 - Los Angeles, California—America's first air meet.

. . . June 13—Walter Brookins sets new altitude record of 5,092 feet in his Wright Flyer.

. . . Sept 2—Blanche Scott, in a Curtiss pusher, is the first woman in America to leave the ground solo.

. . . Sept 16—The first intentional solo flight by a woman in America is made by Bessie Raicle in a home-made Wright-type aircraft.

. . . Sept - Boston Harbor—Ralph Johnstone captures the duration record by flying 3 hrs, 5 min, and 40 sec.

. . . Oct 31—Ralph Johnstone sets world altitude record of 9,714 feet in a Baby Wright Roadster.

. . . Nov 14 - Chesapeake Bay—Eugene Ely takes off from the deck of the Navy cruiser U.S.S. Birmingham.

. . . Nov 1—Ralph Johnstone's death at Overland Park, Colorado is the first in America of a professional flyer.

1911 . . . Jan 26 - San Diego, California—Glenn Curtiss introduces the first practical seaplane in history.

. . . Aug 1—Harriet Quimby becomes the first licensed woman aviator in the United States.

. . . August - Chicago, Illinois—Lincoln Beachey sets altitude record of 11,642 feet.

. . . Sept 23 - Belmont Park, Long Island—Earl Ovington in his Bleroit monoplane flies the first pouch of U.S. Air Mail.

. . . Nov—C.P. Rodgers, flying his Wright-EX biplane, *Vin Fiz*, completes the first coast-to-coast trip across America.

1912 . . . Glenn Curtiss builds his first real flying boat that leads to the construction of the twin-OX engine "*America*" in 1914.

. . . March - St. Louis, Missouri—Captain Bert Berry makes the first parachute descent from an airplane.

. . . June 1—Julia Clark is the first American aviatrix to be killed in an airplane crash.

1913 . . . Glen L. Martin builds a 'Model T' tractor-propeller biplane for the Army's first satisfactory training airplane.

. . . June 21 - Griffin Park, Los Angeles—Georgia 'Tiny' Broadwick, using a Glenn Martin parachute, is the first woman to jump from an airplane, making over 900 more jumps before retiring in 1922.

1914 . . . Lawrence Sperry introduces safety and automatic piloting to aviation with the invention of his gyroscopic stablizer, and later the turn and bank indicator.

. . . World's first scheduled airline began operation with pilot Tony Janus flying a Benoist flying boat on the 22-mile route between St. Petersburg and Tampa, Florida.

1915 . . . Jan 15 - San Diego—One-man duration record set by Lt. B.Q. Jones in a Martin tractor biplane: 8 hrs and 53 min.

. . . July 18 - Cicero Field, Chicago—Katherine Stinson is the first woman in the world to loop-the-loop an airplane.

. . . Nov 19-20—Ruth Law sets three records in a Curtiss pusher with her 590-mile flight in 5 hrs and 45 min.

1917 . . . April 6—The United States enters World War I.

. . . Sept—Ruth Law sets 14,700 altitude record for women.

1918 . . . May 15—official opening of the Aerial Mail Service.

. . . Nov 11—Armistice signed to end World War I.

1919 . . . May—Cmdr. Putty Read and crew of four complete first transatlantic flight with a Curtiss NC-4 flying boat.

. . . Sept 18—Roland Rohlfs in a Curtiss triplane sets altitude record of 31,420 feet.

1920 . . . Eighteen-year-old Ethel Dare is the first woman to change planes in mid-air.

. . . Sept 8—first transcontinental air mail flight.

. . . Nov 25—First Pulitzer race won by Maj. C.S. Moseley with a new speed record of 178 mph.

1921 . . . Feb 21—first transcontinental flight within 24 hours made by Lt. W.D. Coney in a DH-4B from San Diego to Jacksonville, Florida in 22 hrs and 2 min.

. . . July—Gen. 'Billy' Mitchell demonstrates skill of aerial bombing by sinking the German battleship *Ostfriesland.*

1923 . . . May 2-3—first nonstop transcontinental flight made by Lt. Oakley G. Kelly and Lt. John A. Macready in a Fokker T-2; 2,520 miles in 26 hrs and 50 min.

1924 . . . Apr-Sept—Douglas World Cruiser aircraft of the U.S. Army Air Service complete the first round-the-world flight after flying 26,345 miles in 175 days.

. . . July 1—Post Office Department inaugurates continuous air mail service between New York and San Francisco.

1925 . . . Feb—Air Mail Act passed for mail service with private contractors. Ford Air Transport the first to haul mail.

. . . Oct 25—Lt. James Doolittle piloting a Curtiss R3C-2 wins the Schneider Trophy Race with a speed of 232.5 mph.

. . . Dec 17—Gen 'Billy' Mitchell found guilty at court-martial of criticizing the state of U.S. military aviation.

. . . American Robert H. Goddard launches the first rocket.

1927 . . . May 20-21—Charles Lindbergh in his Ryan monoplane, *Spirit of St Louis*, completes the first solo flight across the Atlantic in 33½ hrs.

. . . May 25—Jimmy Doolittle executes the first outside loop in aviation history.

1928 . . . Charles 'Speed' Holman sets a world record of 1433 consecutive loop-the-loops in 5 hrs over St. Paul airport.

1929 . . . ***Ninety-nines*** organization of women pilots organized.

. . . Sept 24—Jimmy Doolittle makes the first blind flight in aviation history

1930 . . . April 20—New transcontinental speed record of 14 hrs and 23½ min set by Charles and Ann Lindbergh.

. . . May—first group of eight stewardesses begin service on Boeing 80A transport for a 20-hr, 13-stop flight from Chicago to San Francisco.

. . . May 8 - St. Louis Lambert Field—Laura Ingalls sets women's record of 344 consecutive loops after 1 hr and 3 min in her DeHaviland Gypsy Moth. On August 14 she breaks Dale Jackson's record of 417 barrel rolls by executing 714 rolls in 3 hrs and 39 min.

1931 . . . Apr 8—Amelia Earhart establishes a woman's auto-giro altitude record of 18,415 feet.

. . . Clyde Pangborn awarded the Harmon Trophy for his non-stop Pacific crossing.

. . . June 23-July 1—Wiley Post and Harold Gatty circle the globe in 8 days, 15 hrs, 51 min in their Lockheed Vega.

1932 . . . May 21-22—Amelia Earhart flying a Lockheed Vega, is the first woman pilot to solo the Atlantic Ocean.

1933 . . . Feb—first flight of the Boeing 247 monoplane airliner.

. . . July 15-22—Wiley Post and his Lockheed Vega "*Winnie Mae*", make the first solo flight of the globe in 7 days, 18 hrs, 49½ min, with seven stops on the 15,596-mile route.

. . . Aug - Curtiss Field, Long Island—Women's endurance record of 196 hrs and 5 min set by Louise Thaden and Frances Marsalis in a Curtiss Thrush.

. . . Sept 3—Maj. Jimmy Doolittle sets a new world speed record for landplanes of 294 mph in a Gee Bee monoplane.

1935 . . . Sept 13 - Santa Ana, California—Howard Hughes shatters all landplane records by flying his *Hughes Special* at 352 mph.

1936 . . . June—Douglas *DC-3* twin-engine aircraft enters service to start its career as the greatest transport aircraft of history.

. . . Oct 24—first transpacific passenger service completed by Pan American Airways with their Martin four-engined "*China Clipper*" in a round trip to Manila.

1938 . . . Aug 22—the Civil Aeronautics Act comes into effect.

1939 . . . Sept—Igor I. Sikorsky makes first successful flight of a single-main-rotor helicopter.

. . . June—first transatlantic passenger service by Pan American Airways with a Boeing four-engined "*Yankee Clipper*".

1947 . . . Charles Yeager breaks the sound barrier in the Bell X-1.

1957 . . . Russia's *Sputnik I* is the first space vehicle to achieve orbit.

1961 . . . Apr 12—Russian astronaut Yuri Gagarin first man to orbit the earth.

1969 . . . July 20—first manned moon landing by U.S. astronauts Neil Armstrong, Edwin Aldrin Jr., and Michael Collins in the Apollo 11 spacecraft. Armstrong, carrying a piece of the original fabric from the Wright Flyer that made history at Kitty Hawk, takes the first step on the moon's surface.

Lincoln Beachey

(b. 1887—d. March 14, 1915)

To the Wright Brothers he was the greatest aviator of all time; no other pilot could match his skill and precision. By 1910, at the age of 23, he had built and operated his own dirigible. Then he started flying with Glenn Curtiss, and went on the exhibition circuit, probably flying more dates in 1911 and 1912 than any other pilot in America.

Believing that the public only wanted to see him kill himself, he quit for a year and went into vaudeville, which was a disaster. But making a flying comeback, he performed the first loop-the-loop in America.

He was back on the circuit to a busier season than ever in 1914. Purchasing a new monoplane, he planned a special show for the Panama-Pacific International Exposition in San Francisco. During the afternoon performance the monoplane went into an uncontrollable dive, snapping the wings off, sending the pilot and machine into the bay. *The Flying Fool* had made his last flight.

Silas Christofferson

(b. 1889 — d. Oct 31, 1916)

A champion stunt flyer of his day, he gained fame with his flight from the roof of Portland's Multnomah Hotel during the 1912 Rose Festival. That fall he married Edna Bissner, and they celebrated with her holding on for dear life through rain squalls during their honeymoon flight.

In 1913 he and his brother started the first scheduled passenger service in California, flying from the waters of San Francisco Bay. They moved to Redwood City in 1914 to give flight instruction and build airplanes for foreign governments.

Conceiving the airplane to be a necessity in modern warfare, Si criticized the United States government for '*sleeping*' in aviation development. Among his accomplishments were distance and altitude records, development of an enclosed fuselage, and overcoming problems with tractor motors pulling an aircraft.

His life ended suddenly in 1916, when he was killed while testing the controls of one of the most advanced designs of the day.

Ann Bohrer

b. Jan 23, 1904

Starting work in December 1927 as an executive secretary for Rankin Aviation of Portland, Oregon, it was only natural that she learn to fly—soloing in a Waco-10 biplane in 1928. Along with her office management job she became public relations director with Portland-Pendleton Airways in the early 1930s. In that capacity, she also became the first stewardess employed in the state of Oregon, flying in the company's 6-passenger Ryan Brougham.

When Tex Rankin moved his operation to California to train cadets for World War II, Ann remained in Portland to work with the U.S. Fish and Wildlife Service, retiring in 1970 after 29 years of service. Although changing careers, she never lost interest in aviation, collaborating with her brother Walt in writing ***Twenty Smiling Eagles***, ***This is Your Captain Speaking***, and ***Tails Up***. Ann is currently working on a new book project, and living in Tualatin, Oregon.

Walt & Nancy Kistler Bohrer

b. May 9, 1909 — b. Jan 13, 1918

Walt started flying at Vancouver, Washington in 1925, working for lessons in lieu of pay, and often skipping school to do so. Soloing in a Curtiss Jenny the following year, he barnstormed for nearly a decade while assisting in the promotion of Rankin Flying Service. He and Tex originated ***Tailspins*** magazine, and Walt went on to head the publicity and help create the ***Rankin System of Flying*** and ***Rankin Text Series*** of aviation books. This started him on a 54-year career as writer, cartoonist, and promoter of aviation, authoring two books on Tex Rankin, feature writing for a variety of aviation magazines, and collaborating with his sister Ann on other book projects.

Nancy first started flying lessons with Walt at Rankin Field in 1934, soloing in a Curtiss Jenny. She quit flying to study education, retiring from teaching physical education after 22 years in the Portland area. She and Walt met shortly thereafter, married, and now live in Tualatin, Oregon, devoting much of their time to promoting aviation and preserving its history.

Glenn Hammond Curtiss

b. May 21, 188 d. July 23, 1930

Born in Hammondsport, New York, Glenn Curtiss showed inventive aptitude early in life, dropping out of school at the age of 14 to start his own bicycle factory. He was soon building motorcycles of his own design and aeronautical motors for Thomas Baldwin's dirigibles. Obsessed with speed, Curtiss was the fastest human in the world by 1907, traveling 136 mph on his motorcycle. He went on to design the *June Bug* pusher biplane which he flew on June 21, 1908, winning his first Scientific American Trophy for flying. In 1909 he set a world air speed record of 47.6 mph during his dramatic victory in the Gordon Bennett Cup race at Rheims, France. This triggered a great demand for his planes and engines, permitting him to start flying schools and manufacture aircraft. Of his flying boats, the largest was his multi-engined "*America*" designed in 1914 for transatlantic flight. By World War I he was the only contractor in the United States ready to build airplanes by the thousands for the U.S. war effort, with his Curtiss *Jenny* becoming the principle WWI training airplane.

Amelia Earhart

b. July 24, 1898 — disappeard July 2, 1937

Born in Atchison, Kansas, Amelia grew up with a hunger for accomplishment and a determination never to be dependent on anyone but herself. After quitting school in 1918 to serve as a nursing aide in a Canadian hospital, she witnessed an aerial exhibition and lost her heart to aviation. Learning from pioneer instructor, Neta Snook, Amelia won international acclaim as the first woman to cross the Atlantic by air—though as a passenger. By 1929 aviation was a full-time career with organizing the Ninety-nines society of women aviators, flying 18,415 feet high in an autogiro, piloting her Lockheed Vega solo across the Atlantic in 1932, crossing America nonstop in 19 hrs and 15 min, and flying from Hawaii to California.

Publisher George Putnam, whom she married in 1931, acted as her publicity manager for these record-breaking excursions, the most remembered being her 1937 around-the-world attempt with navigator Fred Noonan. To this day it is aviation's greatest mystery: what happened to them in the South Pacific?

Danny Grecco

b. Nov 11, 1896 — d. Oct 13, 1983

Equally remembered around his hometown of Portland, Oregon as a fearless barnstormer and master mechanic, Danny Grecco showed interest in aviation at a very early age, building paper balloons which set the neighborhood afire, and building model airplanes. He quit high school to hawk papers, started mechanicing, and then joined the Army Signal Corps in WWI.

After his discharge, Danny went to barnstorming with stunting, parachuting, and wingwalking. His antics of handstands on the top wing of a Jenny, and dangerous plane-to-plane transfers without a parachute were without equal in the Northwest.

He gave up barnstorming to marry his wife Genevieve, but remained in aviation the rest of his life, becoming the first commercial helicopter mechanic in the nation with Bell license number 1. Other recognitions include: "Man of the Year" bestowed in 1959 by the OX-5 Club of Oregon, the "Best Aviator Mechanic in the West" by the FAA in 1968, and induction into the Aviation Hall of Fame in 1973.

Charles K. Hamilton

b. 1886 — d. Jan 22, 1914

Reportedly beginning his flying career with an umbrella jump from a school window in his hometown of New Britain, Connecticut, Charlie was 18 when he left home to take up hot-air ballooning and parachute jumping at exhibitions and circuses across the nation. After becoming one of the most daring parachutists of the era, he started flying dirigibles in 1906, then in 1909 climbed aboard a Curtiss pusher to make several short flights without any lessons.

That November he joined the Curtiss Exhibition Team to tour the nation. Weighing in at 110 pounds, minus the loaded pistol and roll of bank notes he carried in his hip pockets—with red hair, large ears, and the ever-present cigarette dangling from his lips, Hamilton was one of the most colorful characters of the early-day flying pioneers. He stunted with a daring sort of fatalism that awed his fellow pilots and led to more than the usual number of bad crashes, 63 in all, which led to a battered body, but not death until tuberculosis overcame him in 1914.

Dorothy Hester Stenzel

b. Sept 14, 1910 — d. Mar 1, 1991

Born in Milwaukie, Oregon, Dorothy grew up dreaming of adventure, and an airplane ride at the age of 17 led her to flying. She parachuted from a plane to pay for lessons, and soloed with Elrey Jeppesen in 1928. She went on to learn stunt flying under the direction of Tex Rankin, and in 1931 they barnstormed 38 states in a three-month period. During the tour, Dorothy set a still unbroken record for both men and women of 56 inverted snaprolls, and a woman's record of 62 perfect outside loops which remained in place for nearly 60 years.

After opening a flying school in 1932, she settled down to marry Robert Hofer in 1934; but aviation was still in her blood, and in 1948 she was the first woman to take the 'G' test, with readings of 6.3 without a pressure suit, and an 8.6 with one.

Other recognitions were: life membership by the Women's International Assoc. of Aeronautics in 1930, and induction into the OX-5 Aviation Pioneers Hall of Fame in 1980, and the Seattle Museum of Flight Pathfinder Hall of Fame in 1989.

Elrey B. 'Jepp' Jeppesen

b. Jan 28, 1907

Born in Lake Arthur, Louisiana, but growing up in Odell, Oregon, Jepp was fascinated with the birds in flight. Quiting school, he borrowed $500 to buy an old Jenny, then upgraded to an Eaglerock in 1928 to instruct and barnstorm with Tex Rankin. He later flew aerial survey for Fairchild, then air mail for Varney Airways and Boeing. During this time he collected information for let-down procedures to include in his little black book which evolved into the ***Jeppesen Airway Manual.***

In 1936 he married his wife Nadine, a United Air Lines Stewardess, and they moved to Denver in 1941 to continue publishing. After Jepp logged about 10,000 hours with United Air Lines, he left to expand his business, and in 1961 sold out to Times-Mirror which formed the Jeppesen-Sanderson Company to produce the ***Jeppesen Airway Manuals*** which are now used world-wide.

With great recognition, Jepp was inducted into the National Aviation Hall of Fame in 1990. He and Nadine now reside in Englewood, Colorado.

Charles Lindbergh

b. Feb 4, 1902 — d. Aug 26, 1974

Probably the best known figure in aeronautical history was born in Detroit, Michigan, but spent most of his youth in Minnesota and Washington, D.C.. His interest in aviation led to enrollment in flying school, the purchase of a surplus *Jenny*, and barnstorming through the Southern and Midwestern states. After a year at Army flying schools in Texas, he became an air mail pilot in 1926 on the St. Louis-Chicago run. In 1927 he made the record books by flying his Ryan monoplane, *Spirit of St. Louis* cross country in 21 hrs, 20 min; then on May 20th he took off from Roosevelt Field in New York, and landed 33 hrs, 39 min later at Le Bourget Air Field in Paris, for the first solo flight across the Atlantic, making him a world hero.

Marrying Ann Morrow in 1929, the couple made pioneering flights around the world; and during WW-II, 'Lindy' flew combat missions in the Pacific, and then continued consulting after the war was over. Among his hundreds of honors, he was awarded the Medal of Honor by a special act of Congress in 1927.

Ormer Locklear

b. Oct 28, 1891 — d. Aug 2, 1920

Born in Greenville, Texas, Ormer Locklear was a farm boy with a penchant for stunting, first with motorcycles, and then with airplanes after he joined the Army at the age of 26. A lean, hard-muscled bundle of energy, Locklear became internationally famous because of his daring and unusual ability to walk on the wings of planes in flight, but he was more—he was the undisputed king of the daredevils, whose short professional career of only 16 months as a stunt pilot and movie star skyrocked him to unprecedented success. At the height of his career he was making $1,000 a day, and sometimes $3,000, for half an hour's work.

To Locklear, more than anyone else, can be credited the boom in barnstorming that captured America in the 1920s. He made wing-walking a true artform, being the first man in the world to change from one plane to another in mid-air. He lived only for aviation, but it was a short love affair, for he died in a tragic crash during the filming of ***The Skywayman*** on August 2, 1920.

Raoul Lufbery

b. Mar 21, 1885 — d. May 19, 1918

Born in Clermont, France, he was raised by his grandmother, then at the age of 19, he decided to see the world, working on the Continent before reaching Wallingford, Connecticut in 1906 to join the U.S. Army for service in the Philippines. This entitled him to claim American citizenship before visiting the Orient, where he teamed up with French aviator Marc Pourpe to barnstorm Africa and Europe. In 1914 he volunteered for the French Foreign Legion, but then joined the all-American *Lafayette Escadrille* air unit on May 24, 1916. As a pilot he was slow to learn, but soon became one of the most respected aviators on the Western Front. After break-up of the *Escadrille*, he was given a major's commission and assigned to the renown "Hat in the Ring" 94th Squadron, being in charge of training new recruits.

On May 19, 1918 he flew into action with 17 official kills to his credit, but his luck finally ran out and he was shot down in a firefight.

Among his many awards were the Croix de Cuerre, the Me'daille Militaire, and the Legion of Honor.

Frank Luke, Jr.

b. 1897 — d. Oct 1918

Frank Luke grew up in Arizona an undisciplined young man wanting no part of the war, but his sister, who had become a nurse, persuaded him to join U.S. Signal Corps, after which he was accepted for flight training in Texas and California. Commissioned a second lieutenant January 23, 1918, he was sent to France for advanced flying and aerial gunnery training, and then to the 27th Pursuit Squadron at Saintes, France. Being a maverick, he had little use for authority, and oft times disobeyed orders to fly independent missions against the enemy, shooting down ten enemy balloons and four planes in 8 days, a record no other aviator matched, gaining him the reputation as the most daring pilot of the war. On his last flight he was wounded while shooting down three balloons. He landed safely behind enemy lines, but was gunned down when he refused to surrender.

For his bravery, Frank Luke was awarded the Congressional Medal of Honor.

Wiley Post

b. Nov 22, 1899 — d. Aug 15, 1935

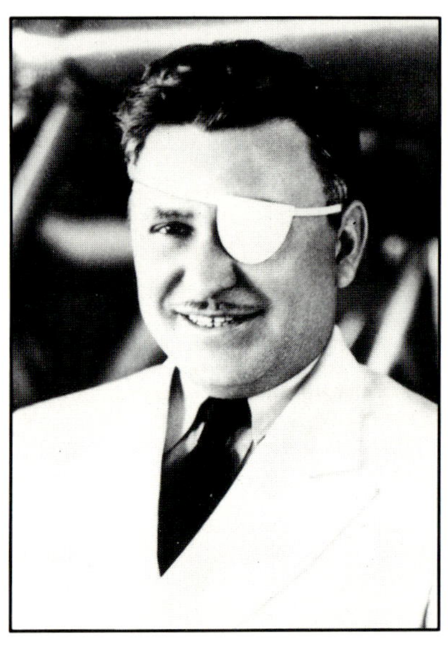

Born in Grand Plain, Texas, Wiley escaped life on the farm by working the oil fields where he lost the sight of his left eye in an accident. With $2,000 from worker's compensation, he invested in a second-hand airplane to begin barnstorming in 1924. He quit the circuit after marrying Mae Laine in 1927, but stayed in aviation, winning the Chicago-Los Angeles Air Derby in 1930. Then, the following year, with Harold Gatty navigating, he circled the globe in the Lockheed Vega, *Winnie Mae*—15,474 miles in 8 days, 15 hrs, 51 min. In 1933, he made one of the most grueling flights in history by flying the *Winnie Mae* solo around the world in 7 days, 18 hrs, 49½ min. In 1935, on a vacation flight with humorist Will Rogers, their lives ended in a crash during takeoff, creating one of the greatest tragedies in American history.

Among Post's numerous awards were the Distinguished Flying Cross, the Collier Trophy, Harmon Trophy, and a F.A.I International Gold Medal for his outstanding feats in aviation.

John Gilbert 'Tex' Rankin

b. 1884 — d. 1947

Born in Brenham, Texas, Tex spent his youth craving adventure. Refused by the Northwest Mounted Police when he was 16, he settled for the National Guard at Walla Walla, Washington, and then served in France during WWI. After the war he learned flying at Spokane, then bought a Curtiss *Jenny* to instruct and barnstorm through southern Idaho. After marrying Shirley Wadsworth in 1921, he continued barnstorming, and then moved to Portland, Oregon to start his own aviation company. Besides instructing, Tex participated in several cross-country air races and performed outstanding aerobatics, including setting a world record of 131 consecutive outside loops in 1931. He was acclaimed top U.S. aerobatic pilot at the National Air Races in 1935, then World Champion in 1937. He opened the Rankin Aeronautical Academy in Tulare, California in 1940, teaching over 10,000 cadets during the war years. After that he formed Rankin Aviation Industries, and continued active until his tragic death in a forced landing at Klamath Falls, Oregon in 1947.

Edward Vernon 'Eddie' Rickenbacker

b. Oct 8, 1890 — deceased

Born to a poor family in Columbus, Ohio, Eddie had to leave school at age twelve to work in a glass factory. Interest in automobiles and a correspondence course in mechanical engineering led him into the world of auto-racing.

After joining the Army, he was the personal chauffeur for Gen. Pershing, but after reaching France, was influenced by Col. Billy Mitchell to join the Air Service. Assigned to the 94th Aero Pursuit Squadron, he downed his first German plane on April 29, 1918. His fifth kill made him an Ace by May 30th. Illness took him out of action for the summer, but he returned in September, and by the 24th he was recognized as the *American Ace of Aces*, promoted to Captain, and assigned to command the *Hat-in-the-Ring* Squadron. By the end of the war, Eddie was the leading American Ace with twenty-six victories in his 134 air battles. In 1930 he was awarded the nation's highest military award—the Congressional Medal of Honor.

He continued with aviation, being appointed president and general manager of Eastern Airlines in 1938, and was still making headlines during WW-II.

Calbraith Perry Rodgers

b. Jan, 1879 — d. Apr 3, 1912

Cal Rodgers was a tall cigar-chomping daredevil who gave up motorcycles to learn flying. After just 90 minutes of instruction at the Wright School, he was ready to solo, and not long afterward won $1,285 grand prize money at the 1911 summer Intn'l Air Meet in Chicago. That fall he set out in a Wright EX biplane named the *Vin Fiz* to claim the $50,000 prize offered by William Randolph Hearst for the first coast-to-coast flight under 30 days. Due to a multitude of calamities and 15 crashes, it took him 49 days to cover 4,231 miles, putting him out of the money, but not out of acclaim as the first pilot to make the transcontinental crossing.

Honored across the land, he received a gold medal from the Aero Club of America, and drew large crowds whenever he flew, but his life was cut short one afternoon when he took off for a quick spin around Long Beach. A flock of seagulls hit his plane, plunging him into the water.

Cal was inducted into the Aviation Hall of Fame in 1964, and the *Vin Fiz* now hangs in the National Air and Space Museum.

Dean C. Smith

b. 1903 — d. Mar 4, 1989

Born in Cove, Oregon, Dean Smith attended Principia Military School in St. Louis, Missouri before joining the Army in 1918. His conniving character got him into cadet school and then commissioned as an Army flight instructor—at age 17, the youngest in Army history. Discharged in 1919, he barnstormed for a short time before signing on with the Aerial Mail Service to pioneer the transcontinental route across the United States. Quitting in 1927, he flew in Antartica as a member of Richard E. Byrd's 1928 expedition. He next joined American Airlines, then went to work for Curtiss-Wright Corp. as a test pilot and sales executive. He quit flying commercially in 1943, but continued working for several aircraft companies.

Dean belonged to the Air Mail Pilots Association and the Quiet Birdmen, as well as being the last president of the National Air Pilots Assoc. Among his awards were the Distinguished Flying Cross and the Harmon Trophy; and he was inducted into the Aviation and OX-5 Halls of Fame.

Katharine Stinson

b. 1898 — deceased

Learning to fly at age 16, with the object of becoming an exhibition flyer to finance a music career, Katharine loved it so much that she gave up her music plans and became one of the greatest exhibition aviators of the era. Being the fourth woman in America to obtain a pilot's license, she was the first woman in the world to loop-the-loop an airplane. She set distance and endurance records with a 9-hr San Diego-San Francisco flight, and a 10-hr Chicago-Binghamton, N.Y. flight.

With their mother as business manager, she and her sister Marjorie started an aviation school in San Antonio, Texas, where they taught their brothers Jack and Eddie to fly. At the outbreak of WWI, she tried enlisting as a military aviator, but was rejected because of her sex. Putting her flying to good use, she raised funds for the Red Cross and Liberty Loan drives, and taught military pilots before she went overseas to serve as an ambulance driver in England and France. While there, she contracted influenza and had to return to the U.S.. Her health worsened and she was forced to retire from aviation in 1920.

Roscoe Turner

b. 1895 — deceased

One of the most colorful pilots of all time was Roscoe Turner, a flamboyant showman with waxed mustache who always flew in military-type uniforms of his own design—his favorite being a powder blue. In 1930, when he began flying for the Gilmore Oil Company whose trademark was a lion, he adopted *Gilmore*, a lion cub to accompany him in the air. The two were inseparable, sharing hotel rooms on the road, registering as *Roscoe and Gilmore*, until *Gilmore* was grounded after 25,000 flying miles because he had grown too large to fit the plane's cabin. For the remaining twenty-five years of his life, Gilmore lived in a small zoo in Los Angeles, and after his death, Turner had him stuffed to remain in his trophy room to share the memories.

Turner was one of the top racers in the country, setting transcontinental speed records in 1932, 1933, and again in 1934; the only three-time winner of the Thompson Trophy Race, with a Wedell-Williams in 1934, then in 1938 and 1939 with his RT-14 Meteor; and the Bendix Race in 1933 and again in 1944.

Jessie Schultz Woods

b. Jan 27, 1909

Jessie was born in Seward, Kansas and spent her early childhood on her father's wheat farm before attending Washington State University. Returning to Kansas, she met Jimmie Woods. They married 1928, and barnstormed their way to Florida, where they purchased several planes, hired pilots, and formed ***The Flying Aces***, to barnstorm the country for the next nine years. Ever increasingly stringent bureaucratic regulations made it tough to survive the circuit, so Jessie and Jimmie locked the doors in 1937, leased the airport at Camden, South Carolina, and Jimmie became chief pilot for Cannon Aircraft while Jessie carried on in aircraft restoration. They trained pilots for WW-II, then leased an airport in Chester until Jimmie's death in 1959. Selling the business, Jessie worked for Washington State, retiring in 1974 to settle in St. Petersburg, Florida. She has since stayed active in aviation with the Ninety-nines, being appointed 3rd Governor in the Southeast Section.

With her approval, ***The Flying Aces*** has been resurrected to carry the thrill of the aerial circus on to new generations.

Orville Wright
b. Aug 19, 1871 — d. Jan 30, 1948

Wilbur Wright
b. Apr 16, 1867 — d. May 30, 1912

Orville and Wilbur Wright were the first to successfully conquer space with a powered craft heavier than air.

As boys in Dayton, Ohio, they showed great inventiveness by making and selling mechanical toys. With no more than high school educations, they went on to printing and publishing a paper, and then engaged in the manufacturing of bicycles from 1892 through 1904. Meanwhile, becoming increasingly interested in the problem of flight, they took a thoroughly scientific approach to building gliders, and flew them at Kill Devil Hill near Kitty Hawk, North Carolina where wind currents provided the most favorable conditions. Back at Dayton, Orville constructed a wind tunnel where they tested hundreds of small models, and by 1903 they were ready to attempt powered flight. At Kill Devil Hill on December 17th, their first flying machine, a biplane powered by a four-cylinder motor and launched by catapult, made four short flights, with the brothers alternating as pilots. With further experimentation, they were able to make a circular flight of 24 miles by the fall of 1905.

Disposing of their bicycle business to devote themselves entirely to building planes, they received a U.S. Patent in May of 1906, and in 1909 they supplied the U.S. Government with her first airplane. Meanwhile, Wilbur had taken one of their aircraft to France, where his successful flights aroused enthusiastic interest, providing for profitable contracts with syndicates in England, France, Germany, and Italy.

The brothers formed the Wright Company for the manufacture of their flying machines, but patent suits plagued them for years, and the worry over the litigations contributed to Wilbur's death in 1912. In 1915 Orville sold his interest in the company, but continued to do research and consulting, serving on the National Advisory Committee for Aeronautics, among other related interests.

Both Orville and Wilbur were recipients of many medals of honor and honorary degrees from the United States and European countries for their recognition in the development of flight. They were both made honorary members of many societies, including: Aeroplane Club of Dayton, Aero Club of U.K., the Aeronautical Societies of America and Great Britain, and the Aero Club of America.

Today, the first Wright Flyer which made history at Kitty Hawk is exhibited at the Smithsonian National Air and Space Museum in Washington, D.C..

Illustrations.....

Original photography by Gildemeister— oil paintings by Tim Larson.

Picture Sources.... **AAHM**—Alaska Aviation Heritage Museum, Anchorage, Alaska; **ISHC**—Idaho State Historical Society, Boise, Idaho; **MOF**—Museum of Flight, Seattle, Washington; **NASM**—National Air and Space Museum, Smithsonian Institution, **OHS**—Oregon Historical Society, Portland, Oregon; **OKHS**—Oklahoma Historical Society, Oklahoma City, Oklahoma.

Illustrations.....

Illustrations.....

Selected Bibliography

***Aviation*—An Historical Survey**.....Charles Harvard Gibbs-Smith, 1970.

Barnstormers and Speed Kings.....Paul ONeil, LC 80-13736.

Barnstorming.....Martin Cadin, LC 65-16275.

***Black Cats and Outside Loops*—Tex Rankin: Aerobatic Ace**.....
Walt Bohrer, LC 89-92104.

By the Seat of My Pants.....Dean C. Smith, LC 61-12809.

***Conquest of the Skies*—A History of Commercial Aviation in America**.....
Carl Solberg, LC 79-15993.

The First Aviators.....Curtis Prendergast, LC 79-25919.

The First to Fly.....Sherwood Harris, 1970.

***Flight in America*—1900-1983**.....Roger E. Bilstein, LC 83-24822.

Flight of the Vin Fiz.....E.P. Stein, LC 84-24521.

Flying the Old Planes.....Frank Tallman, 1973.

***Hollywood Pilot*—The Biography of Paul Mantz**.....Don Wiggins, 1967.

Lindbergh Alone.....Brendan Gill, LC 76-54288.

***Locklear:* The Man Who Walked on Wings**.....Art Ronnie, LC 75-37816.

Pioneers of Flight.....Henry T. Wallhauser, LC 72-83276.

Rickenbacker.....Edward V. Rickenbacker, LC 67-22580.

Smithsonian Studies in Air and Space.....Smithsonian Institute.

Soaring Wings.....George Pamer Putnam, LC 39-27687.

Stunt Flying in the Movies.....Jim and Maxine Greenwood, 1982.

***Tracks Across the Sky*—The Story of the Pioneers of the U.S. Air Mail**.....
Page Shamburger, LC 63-20388.

Upside-down Pangborn.....Carl M. Cleveland, 1978.

***We:* His Own Story**.....Charles A. Lindbergh, 1927.

***Wiley Post*—His "Winnie Mae", and the World's First Pressure Suit**.....
Stanley R. Mohler & Bobby H. Johnson. Smithsonian - 1971.

***Wind and Sand*—The Story of the Wright Brothers at Kitty Hawk**.....
Lynanne Westcott & Paula Degen, LC 83-21501.

Tim Larson

ARTIST

Tim's interest in aviation art started very early in life, around the age of ten when he began drawing schematic views from early-day jet models. Since that time, drawing and modeling various aircraft have evolved from just boyhood fun to avid interest.

His dual occupation of both commercial and fine artist have garnered numerous shows and awards, including: the ***Society of Western Artist's*** best of show in oil painting, and design awards from ***Print*** magazine.

Specializing in antique and vintage periods, Tim enjoys concentrating on the more rarely seen aircraft to bring back a sense of history. "Less art is seen in these areas," he says, "because you just can't go into a hobby shop and buy a plastic model of your subject." And when he does need a model, he builds one himself from scratch, using plans from museums and other vintage sources. Currently, he is putting final touches on a 1913 Deperdussin monoplane in bass and cherry woods for a forthcoming project.

The paintings in ***Avian Dreamer*** illustrate Tim's attention to accuracy and detail both of the aircraft themselves and period dress styles. They also showcase the lifestyles of the times in which these aircraft gained fame and became a part of the rich history of early-day aviation.

Jerry & Cathy Gildemeister

AUTHOR, DESIGNER, PHOTOGRAPHER, PUBLISHER

Jerry and Cathy have created ***Avian Dreamers*** as a lasting tribute to the men and women who pioneered the skies of America. It is their most recent endeavor to preserve our national heritage through imaginative book publishing.

Jerry's fascination with flight first began as a boy while building model airplanes, and watching skywriters performing their skills over his home in Detroit, Michigan. His interest hasn't diminished a bit over the years, and his first '*hands on*' experience came in 1957 as a paratrooper in the U.S. Army, earning his wings with the 82nd Airborne. Since then, he has logged hundreds of hours in the air, spotting for fires while working for the U.S. Forest Service, dropping cargo, and photographing from every angle imaginable. Though he has had many a cold and bumpy ride, he still relishes the opportunity to pull the door off and take to the air for another photographic venture.

Jerry and Cathy live in the sagebrush foothills of the Wallowa Mountains of Northeast Oregon. In addition to their fine-art photography and Bear Wallow publishing, they provide a wide range of consulting, photographic, marketing, design, and publishing services from their home-based studio.

Credits

Writing compilation of narrative, photo illustration, and book design — Jerry Gildemeister.

Oil painting illustrations — Tim Larson

Typography set in Goudy Oldstyle — Gildemeister.

Photographic production — Cathy Gildemeister.

Color separations — Screaming Color of Itasca, Illinois

Text paper — Mead Signature Dull supplied by
West Coast Paper Company of Boise, Oregon.

End Papers — Astroparche Cover supplied by
West Coast Paper Company of Boise, Idaho.

Printing — Dynagraphics, Inc. of Portland, Oregon.

Bindery — Lincoln & Allen Company of Portland, Oregon.

Printed and bound in the United States of America

Library of Congress Cataloging-in-Publication Data

Gildemeister, Jerry, 1934—

Summary:
A tribute to the men and women who pioneered the skies. A collection of historic events, remembrances, original art and photographic illustration creatively blended to preserve the early days of flight in America. Illustrated with original art by Tim Larson, photography by Jerry Gildemeister, and historic images from museum and private collections.

Avian Dreamers

by Jerry Gildemeister: with photography and design by Gildemeister and oil painting illustrations by Tim Larson
p. cm.

Includes bibliographical references.

ISBN 0-936376-07-4 : $45.00

1. Aeronautics — United States — History.

I. Larson, Tim, 1947— . II. Title.

TL521.G55 1991 629.13′00973—dc20 90-85397 CIP

ISBN 0-936376-07-4 . . . . $45.00.

The Bear Wallow Story

The Bear Wallow was formed in 1976 with a commitment to help preserve our Western Heritage through excellence in publication. From the beginning we have strived to carve a niche in the world of book publishing by developing a distinctive style of design—richly blending illustration with storyline, sparing little to offer one-of-a-kind limited printings suitable for any coffee table, library, or classroom. Our goal is to make history interesting and entertaining to readers of all ages while creating editions that are valuable to any collection.

Our first endeavor under the sign of the Bear Paw was in 1978 with the release of ***Rendezvous***, a lavishly illustrated story collection of northeast Oregon history depicting the change in the country since the coming of the white man. In 1980 we released ***Traces***, stories from the last still-living Oregon Trail pioneers who came West by covered wagon. Next, we saw a great need to amass the early history of the Oregon Country—from discovery to settlement, so ***Where Rolls the Oregon*** was developed in 1985 from diaries and other writings of sea voyagers, trappers, mountain men, and pioneers with the storyline sensitively blended with photographic illustration to re-create the mood of the countryside in the early 1800s. In 1987, a letter that was brought to our attention became the catalyst for the creation of ***A Letter Home*** which depicted the early history of the Oregon Trail through the letter, diary excerpts, pioneer writings, photography, and artwork. In 1988 the epic history of the American West was captured with a fascinating collection of short stories combined with a wonderful collection of historic photographs in ***An American Vignette***. A most charming account of two young sisters on an isolated homestead captured our hearts, and in 1989 we released ***Around the Cat's Back***.

Avian Dreamers is our most recent publication to combine artistic innovation with historic accuracy and fine printing to continue our commitment to book publishing as a work of art.

—The Bear Wallow Collection—

Rendezvous............ISBN 0-936376-00-7
Traces............ISBN 0-936376-02-3
Where Rolls the Oregon............ISBN 0-936376-03-1
A Letter Home............ISBN 0-936376-04-X
An American Vignette............ISBN 0-936376-05-8
Around the Cat's Back............ISBN 0-936376-06-6

In Parting

I wish to extend a very special thank you to Eugene Clay; without his sparking of my interest, this project would never have 'left the ground'!

And thanks to all others who have so generously assisted, and shared personal experiences, photo collections, and source materials, especially: Hugh Ackroyd, Ann Bohrer, Walt and Nancy Bohrer, Timothy Cronen of the National Air and Space Museum, Bill Doty, Genevieve Grecco, E. B. Jeppesen, Joanne Nelson of E.O.S.C interlibrary loan, Art Ronnie, Ann Rutledge of the Seattle Museum of Flight, Ted Spencer of the Alaska Aviation Heritage Museum, Bob Synoground, Ray Wagner of the San Diego Aerospace Museum, Jessie Woods, and belatedly..... Dorothy Hester Stenzel who left us before this book was completed.

Furthermore, I am indebted to my wife, partner, and co-worker, Cathy, who has made this project possible. Above all, I am especially grateful for the long hours she has endured in the darkroom to create the photographic imagery. Only through her dedication and craftsmanship has it been possible to maintain high quality in this lasting tribute to the men and women who pioneered the skies of America.

Jerry Gildemeister